Jesus and the Poor

Jesus and the Poor

RICHARD BATEY

1817

HARPER & ROW, PUBLISHERS
New York • Evanston • San Francisco • London

FIRST EDITION

LIBRARY OF CONGRESS CATALOG CARD NUMBER: 70–160637

Designed by C. Linda Dingler

To
Evelyn Evon, Richard Edgar, and Helen Kay,
hostages to fortune who enrich my life

Contents

Preface

The subject of this book is the relevance of the understanding and care of the poor in the early church for present concerns with poverty. In recent years few problems in the United States have loomed larger in the national consciousness than the plight of the poor. A number of evident influences contribute to this growing consciousness: (1) The unequaled period of economic growth in the last two decades has not brought prosperity to all alike, but rather has widened the gap between the "haves" and "have nots." (2) Since poverty is generally measured by relative economic conditions, the juxtaposition of rich and poor has intensified awareness on both sides. (3) Greater affluence has provided the capacity to attack the problems of the poor and declare war on those causes that produce or contribute to poverty. (4) Exponents of the poor have arisen, like Moses, to champion their cause and awaken the national conscience. (5) Legislators have passed in rapid succession sweeping social reforms directed toward alleviating the suffering of the poor. (6) In many quarters churchmen have identified with the underprivileged and have redirected and rededicated both their own efforts and those of their churches to aid the needy.

However, the concern for the disfranchised and the numerous programs initiated to alleviate their condition have not produced anticipated success. The difficulties are in large measure due to the fact that the poor are *people*. The technological American know-how, which has proved so successful in the production of household goods, armaments, and spacecrafts, becomes relatively inefficient when dealing with a man in need. The problem of an effective and constructive means of assisting the poor is requiring a rethinking of goals and a restructuring of programs.

The necessity to deal constructively with these problems calls for a reinvestigation of our heritage in order to gain fresh insights into our present situation. A major influence in shaping the values and attitudes of Western man—even secular man— has been an exceptional concern for the weak and oppressed. Although Nietzsche was highly critical of this "slave mentality," which hindered the arrival of his superman, he was entirely correct in seeing preoccupation with the weak and oppressed as central to both Judaism and Christianity.

An initial impression may be that this book is an attempt to return to the "social gospel" that began in America a century ago. But such an anachronism would be untenable today. The idealism and optimism that characterized liberal theology and the "social gospel" in the late nineteenth century have long since passed from the American scene; the conviction that the church through social action will bring in the Kingdom of God on earth is a relic of the past. Also, the recent emphasis on Jewish apocalypticism as the matrix of Christian theology manifests that the ethical teachings of Jesus and the early apostles were not eternal and relevant for every social crisis. On the contrary, the radical ethic of the New Testament was predicated on the conviction that time had grown short and that immediate and decisive action was mandatory. However, the apocalyptic outlook did not lead these Christians to withdraw from the world and human misery; rather the crisis precipitated by the *Endzeit* freed them to deal directly with basic human needs in their community. Their program of caring for the poor arose in a situation of crisis where lack of time demanded radical and immediate response to their God's demands and their brother's need.

Many people have contributed to the completion of this book.

I wish to acknowledge my indebtedness to the Faculty Committee for Research and Creative Activity of Southwestern at Memphis for supporting this project through its program of summer research grants. To my students I especially want to express my gratitude for their enthusiasm in classes on the Christian understanding of the poor and for being both eyes and ears by encountering and reacting to present conditions of poverty. Annie May Alston has graciously read the manuscript and made indispensable stylistic criticisms. Competent secretarial assistance has been provided by Mrs. Sue Henderson and Mrs. Jane Tomlinson. My wife, Carolyn, has continued to lend encouragement by offering helpful suggestions for the manuscript, pleasantly enduring my erratic writing schedule, and making home a joyful haven from the demands of composition.

Scriptural quotations are from the Revised Standard Version of the Bible, copyright 1946 and 1952 by the Division of Christian Education of the National Council of Churches of Christ in the U.S.A. and used by permission.

I

Introduction

While virtually every great culture has had its oppressed
classes whose labor and toil made possible the ease enjoyed
by the more privileged, the study of civilizations generally
focuses on the achievements of those in the upper echelon
of society. The brilliant advances accomplished by Babylon,
Egypt, Greece, and Rome could not have been attained except for the suppression and exploitation of thousands of
slaves and forced laborers. Generally, when one reflects on
the Golden Age of Athens, he is not preoccupied with the
condition of the slaves who actually outnumbered the free
men of this polis. These slaves did the work that provided
leisure for the free citizens to enjoy art and philosophy and
experiment with the democratic process. Even poverty
among the free men was not a primary concern of these lovers of the arts; Thucydides aptly summarized their view
when he had Pericles say in the Funeral Oration: "To avow
poverty with us is no disgrace: the true disgrace is in doing
nothing to avoid it" (*History of the Peloponnesian War*, 40).

However, for Jews the memory of their bondage in Egypt
and the birth of their nation at the Exodus gave them a special interest in the suffering of the poor. The Hebrew prophets continually called out for social justice for their exploited
fellow Israelites. It is in the tradition of these prophets that

Jesus of Nazareth came preaching good news to the poor (Isa. 61:1–2; Luke 4:18–19).

Jesus himself arose from the lower ranks of society and came from a hill town in Galilee well known for its failure to achieve mediocrity (John 1:46). When he left the carpenter's bench to become a rabbi, a teacher in Israel, his economic condition did not improve, since rabbis received no remuneration for their instruction. It was probably no idle figure of speech when Jesus said, "Foxes have holes, and birds of the air have nests; but the Son of man has nowhere to lay his head" (Luke 9:58; Matt. 8:20). His message and ministry were directed largely toward those on the fringe of society: the weak and infirm, the poor, the *am ha'aretz* (the people of the land), and sinners. He declared that "those who are well have no need of a physician, but those who are sick; I came not to call the righteous, but sinners" (Mark 2:17; Matt. 9:12–13; Luke 5:31–32). These common people received joyfully Jesus' message that the Kingdom of God was at hand. This coming reign of God would upset their present standard of values and order of priorities; men from both the east and west would sit at table in the kingdom and the native Jew thrust out (Matt. 8:11; Luke 13:29); even tax collectors and harlots would gain entry before the so-called religious and respectable (Matt. 21:31,32), and the rich and full would become acquainted with want and hunger, while the poor would be blessed in the realization that the Kingdom of God was theirs (Luke 6:20–26). The apocalyptic disruption that would characterize the kingdom's arrival not only called to account the Jew's judgment concerning race and religion, it also contained the seeds of economic revolution and social reversal. While the imminent new age would arrive only by God's power, men were challenged to accept its promise through the acceptance of its radical demand, a demand that did not separate one's spiritual good from his worldly goods (Matt. 19:16–30; Mark 10:17–31; Luke 18:18–30). Those who embraced the promise of the kingdom enjoyed the full fellowship that this hope afforded. An expression of the nature and extent of this fellowship is seen in Jesus and his closest disciples sharing a common purse (John 12:6, 13:29).

After the Crucifixion, Jesus' followers in Jerusalem kept alive the spirit of fellowship and sharing that they had experienced with him. Together they anticipated the parousia when his return would accompany the final realization of the kingdom. Enthused by this prospect and unified by the apostles' teaching, they sought to minister to the needs of the poor in their number. Those with possessions voluntarily sold them, and from these funds daily distributions were made to their needy brethren (Acts 2:44-47, 4:32-37). The messianic proclamation of the first Christians fired the imagination of many for whom hope had burned dim. Those who had the least to lose responded to this message of hope and these acts of charity. Jerusalem contained a large number of poverty-stricken Jews, many of whom had come to the Holy City to die. Soon the needs of the primitive church outran its ability to serve. The crisis resulting from its concern to care for the poor was among the first specific challenges for the early church to understand itself and the implications of the kerygma. This crisis antedates the problems of the relationship of Judaism to Christianity, the relation of Jewish and Gentile Christianity, and the problems arising from the delay of the parousia. Though the care for the poor had a significant influence on these subsequent controversies, it was an initial difficulty that shaped the course of the earliest Christian history.

The degree to which the Jerusalem poverty program affected the history of the church is more obvious when one recognizes that the missionary travels of the apostle Paul were also fundraising campaigns for "the poor among the saints at Jerusalem" (Rom. 15:26). Their condition became so critical that their leaders—Peter, James the brother of Jesus, and John the son of Zebedee—agreed to approve Paul's missionary work among the Gentiles, which was under attack in several quarters; Paul reciprocated by "remember[ing] the poor" (Gal. 2:10). His col-

lection among the Gentile churches that he had founded had
not only the practical result of bringing relief to those Christians
suffering in Jerusalem, even more, the collection helped to
legitimize the status of the Gentile churches in the eyes of
Jewish Christians. It was, therefore, a token of the unity of the
whole *corpus Christi.*

The funding and administration of the poverty program
among the first Christians lies close to the heart of their self-
understanding. The growth of the church in the areas of theology, missions, polity, and the relation of Jewish and Gentile
Christianity cannot be assessed properly apart from an understanding of programs to care for the poor. An historical investi-
gation of their methods and purposes offers not only the opportunity to grasp more clearly the origins of Christianity but also
may indirectly cast new light on contemporary social problems.

Historical research generally is undertaken in response to
problems arising within a culture that require a fresh investiga-
tion of its heritage. The particular problem provides the historian with his principle of selection and specific perspective.

The method for reconstructing the history of the poverty
program of the early Christians is intricate, due to the very
nature of the sources with which one must deal. The reader will
be spared much of the tedium that delights the specialist in the
field. While critical questions cannot be avoided, they will be
dealt with primarily in the notes.[1]

II

Jesus and the Poor

1. Jesus' Social Class

Jesus was a poor man. This impression is deeply stamped on the memory of the early church preserved in the Gospels. While the nativity story in Luke should be understood primarily as theological narrative, it presents Jesus as coming into humble surroundings.[1] Mary and Joseph were unable to obtain lodging in Bethlehem at the inn in spite of their tiresome journey and Mary's advanced pregnancy. They were compelled by the over-crowded conditions to seek shelter in the stable. It was here that Jesus is said to have been born, wrapped in swaddling cloths, and laid in the manger (Luke 2:7). Luke underscores the theme of poverty by suggesting that the offering for purification made by Mary and Joseph at the Jerusalem temple was a "pair of turtledoves, or two young pigeons"; this was the offering pre-scribed by the law for those too poor to afford a lamb (Luke 2:24; cf. Lev. 12:6–8).

Jesus of Nazareth hailed from a little village nestled in the hills of Galilee just north of the broad plain of Esdraelon. Nazareth, fifteen miles from the Sea of Galilee and twenty miles from the Mediterranean, enjoyed a moderate climate due in part to its elevation 1,300 feet above sea level. Lying off the main highway, this village was considered unimpressive and

backward. For example, when Nathanael heard that Jesus was
from this hamlet, his immediate response was, "Can anything
good come out of Nazareth?" (John 1:46). It is not surprising
that Nazareth is not mentioned in the Old Testament, Talmud,
Midrash, or Josephus.

In this village Jesus grew up as the eldest son of Joseph the
carpenter, whose trade had to provide a livelihood for his growing family, four sons besides Jesus—James, Joses, Judas, and
Simon—and at least two daughters (Mark 3:31, 6:3).[2] As was
customary in Judaism, Jesus was an apprentice to his father and
learned the strenuous skills of the woodworker. The details
concerning Jesus' life preserved in the Gospels are meager and
his biography can not be written based on this sketchy information. However, an important question is raised by the fact that
Joseph is not mentioned as being present during the ministry
of Jesus. When Jesus was dying on the cross he placed his
mother Mary in the care of the beloved disciple, who took her
to his own home and provided for her (John 19:26–27). This
suggests that Joseph died when Jesus was a young man, which
is more generous than to speculate that he had abandoned his
family. If indeed Joseph were dead—and arguments from silence must be regarded with caution—Jesus as the eldest son
would have found it his responsibility to provide for a large
family without a father.[3]

Jesus was baptized by John the Baptist and approved the
general direction taken by John's preaching. John's demand for
repentance because the Kingdom of Heaven was at hand (Matt.
3:2) contained implicitly the seeds for social change. To those
with two coats and food the challenge was thrown down to
share with him who had none. John admonished tax collectors
to be honest and commanded soldiers not to rob by violence or
deceit and to be satisfied with their pay (Luke 3:10–14). Mercy
and justice were characteristics of the coming kingdom. Later,
when John had been imprisoned, he sent to ask Jesus if he were
the anticipated messiah. Jesus told John's disciples to go and tell

him what was transpiring: the sick were healed and the poor
had good news proclaimed to them (Luke 7:22). These were
genuine signs of both the identity of Jesus and the arrival of the
Kingdom of God.

At about the age of thirty Jesus began his ministry with the
proclamation of the nearness of the Kingdom of God (Luke
3:23). He assumed the role of a rabbi, but was not as other rabbis
whose erudite teachings were founded on complicated citations
of those authorities whose legal judgments had been preserved
by oral transmission. Jesus taught with a personal authority and
simple directness that distinguished him from the rest and commanded the attention of his hearers, if not their respect (Mark
1:22; Matt. 7:28–29; Luke 4:32). But in one significant respect
Jesus shared the plight of other rabbis: He received no pay for
his teaching and was without visible means of support. He described his condition by saying, "Foxes have holes, and birds of
the air have nests; but the Son of man has nowhere to lay his
head" (Luke 9:58; Matt. 8:20). Joachim Jeremias reckons scholars in Judaism generally to have been among the poorer class
and gives examples from the second century of their miserable
condition.[4] R. Gamaliel II, who was renowned for his great
learning, had not a bite to eat nor a garment to wear (b. Hor.
10a); R. Akiba and his wife were so poor they slept in straw in
the winter (b. Ned. 50a); and the most often quoted rabbi in the
Mishnah, R. Judah b. Eli, possessed only one cloak which he and
his wife wore alternately when they went out (b. Ned. 49b-50a).

The Gospels are consistent in their portrayal of Jesus as one
of the poorer class. As he walked through the fields of standing
grain he pulled off the heads of grain, rubbed them in his hands,
and ate the raw kernels (Mark 2:23–28; Matt. 12:1–8; Luke 6:1–5).
This was in keeping with the humanitarian laws to protect the
poor set down in the Deuteronomic Code (Deut. 23:25). The
law permitted a man to pluck the ears of grain from his neighbor's field but he could not use a sickle.[5] Returning from Beth-
any to Jerusalem in the last week of his life, Jesus was again

foraging. On the road without breakfast he was hungry and turned aside to a fig tree for something to eat. But, finding only leaves, he cursed it (Mark 11:12–14; Matt. 21:18–19).

In this connection it is well to notice the occasions when Jesus' teachings took the form of table talks while he was a guest in someone's home. For example, it was in the home of Martha that Jesus commended her sister Mary for her attentiveness to his teaching. Martha was piqued at Mary's failure to help with the serving and asked Jesus to tell Mary to help. But, Jesus replied, "Martha, Martha, you are anxious and troubled about many things; one thing is needful. Mary has chosen the good portion, which shall not be taken away from her" (Luke 10:41). He also instructed his disciples, when he sent them out to proclaim the message of the kingdom, to live by the hospitality of the righteous (Mark 6:7–13; Matt. 10:5–13; Luke 9:1–6, 10:1–12; cf. Luke 22:35–38). Capernaum by the Sea of Galilee was the setting for the episode concerning the half-shekel temple tax. Before Jesus paid the tax collectors he had to send Peter fishing to procure the money (Matt. 17:24–27). On yet another occasion, when asked if it were lawful to pay taxes to Caesar, Jesus asked to be brought a coin before he would answer (Mark 12:13–17; Matt. 22:15–22; Luke 20:20–26). An indication of Jesus' economic status is also to be found in his traveling on foot; even when he made his triumphal entry into Jerusalem he had to borrow an ass on which to ride (Mark 11:1–10; Matt. 21:1–9; Luke 19:28–38; John 12:12–15).[6]

It was not unusual for students to contribute to the support of their teacher as their meager means would allow. When Jesus launched his ministry in Galilee he was accompanied by a number of women who provided for his needs from their own resources as well as for the twelve. Among this number were Mary Magdalene, Joanna, who was the wife of Chuza, Herod's steward, Susanna (Luke 8:1–4), Mary the wife of Clopas, and Salome (Mark 15:40–41; Matt. 27:55–56; John 19:25). These women left their homes in order to follow Jesus and share their substance with him.[7] One cannot but speculate on the impression such a company would have made descending on a Galilean village, proclaiming the arrival of the Kingdom of God. The charity they gave to Jesus and the twelve was a hallmark of the new age. This sense of sharing joy and goods was a distinctive feature of those who were closest to Jesus. The twelve who had left all to follow Jesus supplied their needs from a common purse that Judas administered (John 12:6, 13:29).[8]

2. The Finger of God

The conduct of Jesus in ministering to the poor, sick, and rejected of society provided the context in which his preaching of the kingdom was to be heard. Luke (4:16–21) introduced this ministry with Jesus' appearance in the Nazareth synagogue one Sabbath and his reading from the Book of Isaiah (61:1–2; cf. Luke 7:22): "The Spirit of the Lord is upon me, because he has anointed me to preach good news to the poor. He has sent me to proclaim release to the captives and recovering of sight to the blind, to set at liberty those who are oppressed, to proclaim the acceptable year of the Lord." Then Jesus said, "Today this scripture has been fulfilled in your hearing." The focus of Jesus' attention came to rest on those disfranchised by society; he was derided as a friend of tax collectors and sinners, but replied that "those who are well have no need of a physician, but those who are sick; I came not to call the righteous, but sinners" (Mark 2:13–17; Matt. 9:9–13; Luke 5:27–32; cf. Luke 7:34, 15:1–2). He ministered to those with a withered hand, a twisted spine, to the lame, palsied, fevered, blind, demented, and lepers clothed in their rags and hopelessness.

In the first century sickness and poverty went hand in hand, because the ill or infirm could not earn a livelihood and were often reduced to begging. It was not unknown for the sick to suffer much from the treatment of many physicians who were unable to heal but who nevertheless charged their fees. Such persons, exhausted physically and financially, also sank among the ranks of the poor (Mark 5:25–34; Matt. 9:20–22; Luke 8: 43–48). A further burden borne by the poor and sick was that many held their misfortune to be the result of divine disapproval due to sin—either their own or that of their parents. And in the prevailing view illness was a manifestation of demon possession. Sin and sickness were, therefore, closely linked in the understanding of that day. Society could then excuse itself for being indifferent toward their needs.

Jesus' ministry was both a sign of the kingdom's arrival and a definition of the quality of life to be lived there. In his compassion to society's outcasts he affirmed the presence of the divine mercy: "But if it is by the finger of God that I cast out demons, then the kingdom of God has come upon you" (Luke 11:20; Matt. 12:28).[9] He proclaimed release for those oppressed by social injustice and prejudice. He attacked the doctrine of retribution, which held man's misfortunes to be divine punishment and declared that God sends the rain on the just and unjust and the sunshine on the evil and the good (Matt. 5:45). The eighteen men who were killed when the tower of Siloam fell were no worse than others; nor were those Galileans whose blood Pilate mingled with their sacrifice any worse than other Galileans (Luke 13:1–5). The beggar's blindness was due to neither his sin nor the sin of his parents (John 9:1–3). But his blindness offered others the opportunity to show mercy and manifest the works of God.[10]

Not only did Jesus reject the current belief that adversity was the result of sin, he proclaimed that God's mercy and forgiveness were available to sinners. So his healing and declaration of forgiveness were two sides of the same shield (Matt. 9:1–8; Mark 2:1–12; Luke 5:17–26). His followers remembered him as one whose compassion prompted him to respond to human suffering where he found it and to redeem life (Matt. 9:36, 14:14, 15:32, 20:34; Mark 1:41, 6:34, 8:2; Luke 7:13; cf. Luke 10:33, 15:20). His works stood in sharp contrast to those physicians whose efforts to heal were in return for payments received (Mark 5:26; cf. Acts 8:18–24). To the twelve he instructed when he sent them out to proclaim that the Kingdom of Heaven was at hand: "Heal the sick, raise the dead, cleanse lepers, cast out demons. You received without pay, give without pay" (Matt. 10:8).

3. Proclamation of the Kingdom

The ministry of Jesus provided in a specific way the sign of the arrival of the kingdom. His proclamation of the kingdom was the declaration that the reign of God was one in which mercy and acceptance would win out over the forces of evil in the world. That divine intervention for which other apocalyptists yearned—when God would crush with cataclysmic might the demonic forces—was no longer to be anticipated as an excuse for failing to acknowledge God's present sovereignty over mankind. The end had arrived—not because time had run out, but because God had come near. And his nearness was sensed in the merciful acts of Jesus. Since the kingdom would come by God's power, its arrival was not dependent on human effort nor could its coming be predicted by the usual means of prognostication (Luke 17:20; Matt. 16:1–4, 24: 3–8, 32–35). Its appearance would be met with a sense of surprise, for it would be detected as one is startled by a thief in the night (Matt. 24:36–44) or as an abusive servant is shocked by his master's unexpected return (Matt. 24:45–51; cf. Matt. 25:1–13). Jesus himself disavowed knowledge of its exact time of arrival (Matt. 24:36), but he was convinced that the Kingdom of God was incipient. He told his listeners that "there are some standing here who will not taste death before they see the kingdom of God come with power" (Mark 9:1; Matt. 16:28; Luke 9:27). One must therefore be circumspect or watchful in order to detect the presence of the kingdom (Matt. 24:42–44, 25:13) "for behold, the kingdom of

God is in the midst of you" (Luke 17:21). Its power and presence
would initially be small and deceptive by the means men usu-
ally measure historical events. But like leaven hidden in meal
or a tiny mustard seed planted in the ground, it would grow to
produce astonishing results (Matt. 13:31–33; Luke 13:18–21).[11]

That the kingdom was from God meant that it would not be
built by human ingenuity and organization. The Zealots, those
political revolutionaries within Judaism who sought by social
turmoil and political intrigue to regain Jewish independence
from the Romans, should not confuse their goals with the kingdom that Jesus proclaimed. Jesus resisted attempts inspired by
the hope of political freedom to make him king (John 6:15). His
kingdom was not of this world, in the sense that it would be
based upon the military power that sustains political states;
consequently, he forbade his followers to resort to violence
(Matt. 26:47–52; Luke 22:49–51; John 18:11, 33–38; cf. Luke 22:
36).[12] The cohesive power of the kingdom would not rest on the
efficient organization of its members. To those aspiring to high
office and authority he replied that to sit on his right hand or
left hand in the kingdom was not his to grant. Greatness in
God's kingdom was not to be measured by one's authority but
by one's compassion. The great would be the servants (Mark
10:35–45; Matt. 20:20–28; cf. Matt. 19:28; Luke 18:28). The cohesive power of the kingdom would be that mercy for the weak
that Jesus displayed and claimed was from God. "Be merciful,
even as your Father is merciful" (Luke 6:36; cf. Matt. 5:48).

To say that the kingdom was not of this world should not be
understood as meaning that the kingdom would be other-
worldly. There were many apocalyptists within Judaism who
had given up hope for the present age, which they were convinced was in the control of demonic powers. The hope of these
visionaries was grounded in the belief that someday God would
intervene in human history with cataclysmic might and destroy
the ruling forces of evil. Following this social and political
upheaval the utopian state would be established. Much apoca-

lyptic literature was preoccupied with blueprinting what the last days, the eschaton, would be.[13] Among canonical Christian literature the Apocalypse of John typifies this perspective. While Jesus shared the apocalyptists' conviction that God was breaking into history, his teachings concerning the Kingdom of God were surprisingly free of such visions and detailed predictions. Instead of God's action being in some remote future day, Jesus declared that God's reign was imminent and that joy should characterize those who anticipated its full appearance. For Jesus membership in the kingdom was conditioned by one's compassion for others. Matthew presented a reinterpretation of apocalyptic views of the coming reign of God. When the Son of Man should come in his glory and sit upon this throne as judge of all nations, the test of membership would be: Have you cared for the least of these, my brethren? Those blessed who would inherit the Father's kingdom would be none other than those who gave food to the hungry, drink to the thirsty, hospitality to strangers, clothes to the naked, and comfort to the sick and imprisoned (Matt. 25:31–46).[14] These deeds were Jesus' deeds and his ministry was a denial of escape from the present evil age in order to dream passively an other-worldly vision. The mercy he revealed was divine, but it afforded no excuse for turning one's back on present human need.

Jesus saw a radical change taking place in the existing social order, and to this extent he was in agreement with the apocalyptist. But the power to effect this transformation was the mercy of God shared in that community that accepted Jesus' life as authentic. The demands of the kingdom were therefore radical because its coming required one to evaluate his life in terms of mercy, not might—either political or economic. It demanded that one sever himself from his old accomplishments and values—leaving father and mother, lands and houses—in order to enter. The kingdom must be received like a little child who stands open to present possibilities and hopeful of future potentialities. It would come to those who trusted that authen-

tic human life was found in that community that reflects compassion, i.e., grace that goes beyond the demands of strict justice to grant acceptance and assistance that one may not justly
claim.

4. The Poor Had Good News

In the theocratic Jewish state of the first century no sharp
distinction was made between religious and civil laws. Religious
convictions afforded the understanding of community and justice that were to be approximated by legal decision and social
customs. The Law of Moses was considered by the devout Jew
to regulate all of life, and meticulous care was taken by scholars
to explicate its relevance for even the most insignificant deeds.
Jesus could not, therefore, criticize the religious practices of his
day without raising social and economic issues. The cleansing of
the temple became for the Gospel writers a sign of the far-
reaching reform that Jesus' ministry inaugurated.[15] When Jesus
drove the money-changers and their customers from the temple, his call for reform—for God's house, which had become a
den of robbers, to be a house of prayer—caused fear in the
Jewish leaders, who recognized at once the threat that his action presented to their position of control. They then sought to
destoy him (Matt. 21:12–13; Mark 11:15–19; Luke 19:45–48; John
2:13–22). The economics of the kingdom were radical because
they challenged the current unjust society by demanding that
men put first the Kingdom of God and his righteousness. Luke,
of all the Gospel writers, is most concerned with this aspect of
Jesus' teaching.

You Cannot Serve God and Mammon

Jesus proclaimed that the demands of the kingdom were radical because they required that one evaluate his life in terms of
mercy and compassion rather than power and wealth. "For

what does it profit a man, to gain the whole world and forfeit
his life?" (Mark 8:36; Matt. 16:26; Luke 9:25). To enter the kingdom one had to be willing to trust himself fully to the future
that God was bringing and to sever himself from entangling
alliances—to cut off his hand or pluck out his eye (Mark 9:43–48;
Matt. 5:29–30, 18:7–9). To participate in the dawning new age
he had to give up all in order to belong to a community that
acknowledged and shared the sovereign mercy of God. For the
Kingdom of Heaven was like a man who sold everything he
possessed in order to purchase a field in which a treasure lay
buried or to buy an exquisite pearl. Radical loyalty was the cost
of discipleship, and the resulting conflict would find expression
even within the family circle; but the bond of the kingdom was
stronger than familial ties (Matt. 10:34–38; Luke 12:51–53, 14:
26–27).

Jesus' disciples were not to confuse what a man is with what
he has, because "a man's life does not consist in the abundance
of his possessions" (Luke 12:15). To that man seeking Jesus' assistance in obtaining a share of the family estate, Jesus warned
against covetousness. He told a parable about a rich farmer
whose fields were so productive that he had no place to store
his surplus. So he tore down his old barns and constructed larger
storage houses to contain his wealth. Then, with a deep sense
of self-satisfaction, he said, "Soul, you have ample goods laid up
for many years; take your ease, eat, drink, be merry" (Luke
12:19). But death ended his retirement that very night. This
man, diligent in planning, industrious in sowing and reaping,
and frugal in the preservation of his wealth, was judged a fool,
because he valued his life by material wealth instead of being
rich toward God. Jesus saw the acquisitive spirit as preventing
men from entering wholly into the kingdom. Like thorns growing among the grain, the delight in riches and the cares of the
world choked their life. To Jesus the issue was clear, for no man
could serve two masters; "You cannot serve God and mammon"
(Luke 16:13; Matt. 6:24).

This choice was made obvious to the rich young man who came to Jesus asking, "Good Teacher, what must I do to inherit eternal life?" (Mark 10:17–23; Matt. 19:16–23; Luke 18:18–24). Learning that the man had kept the moral demands of the decalogue from his youth, Jesus looked at him with genuine affection and replied, "You lack one thing; go, sell what you have, and give to the poor, and you will have treasure in heaven; and come, follow me" (Mark 10:21). But the young man went away dejected because he had great possessions and yet could not pay the price of surrendering all. This young man, an exemplary son of the law, virtuous and conscientious, cared more for his possessions than for life in the kingdom.[16] Jesus was left to remark to his disciples, "How hard it will be for those who have riches to enter the kingdom of God!" (Mark 10:23). In response to their amazement at this hard saying, Jesus further perplexed them with the repartee: "It is easier for a camel to go through the eye of a needle than for a rich man to enter the kingdom of God" (Mark 10:25).[17]

In marked contrast to this encounter was the response of Zacchaeus, a chief tax collector and a member of that despised group of Jews who worked hand in glove with the Roman authorities to fleece their own fellow countrymen (Luke 19:1–10). Zacchaeus was rich. Being short and wishing to see Jesus over the crowd, he climbed a sycamore. Here Jesus greeted Zacchaeus and informed him that he would be Jesus' host that day. Joyfully Zacchaeus escorted Jesus to his home, leaving others to murmur, "He has gone in to be the guest of a man who is a sinner." But this chief of sinners was convicted by his guest and volunteered, "Behold, Lord, the half of my goods I give to the poor; and if I have defrauded any one of anything, I will restore it fourfold." To which Jesus replied that salvation had come to his house that very day.[18]

Discipleship meant that one placed first the new righteousness that Jesus taught. Compassion for others, not greed, was to become the basis of the new economy. Those with riches were

challenged to distribute to others as God's mercy and human
needs dictated. In a world where avarice was the rule of the
day, where even many religious leaders were known to be
lovers of money (Luke 16:14) whose show of piety and eleemosynary acts were calculated to impress the observer (Matt 6:1–4),
Jesus called for deeds reflecting genuine justice and mercy
(Matt. 23:23; Luke 11:42–43). He was often critical of the form
of religion without the spirit of love. He castigated those hypocrites whose pious religious observances were without mercy as
well as those who used religion to enhance their social status
(Matt. 23:1–36). To be in the kingdom meant having faith in the
sovereignty of a compassionate Father and reflecting his sovereignty within the unjust social order. The obdurate acquiring
and possession of wealth in the midst of human misery and
suffering is evil in itself, because it is a rejection of this compassion. Jesus' admonition was not to lay up treasures on earth, but
to seek first the Kingdom of God; material things would then
come in their proper place (Matt. 6:33; Luke 12:31). In the Gospels Judas was the prime example of one who had misplaced his
values, betraying his friend and master for thirty pieces of silver
(Matt. 27:3–9).

To the poor and common people Jesus affirmed their accepta-
bility before God. They were not to consider their lack of health
and wealth as a sign of divine disapproval, for indeed, of their
numbers the ranks in the kingdom would be filled. But Jesus
warned them against making the same mistake as the rich.
They, too, could not consider the possession of goods as the true
measure of life. He challenged them not to be preoccupied with
physical needs, for which deprivation often created an obses-
sion. Anxiety about food and clothing does not portray that
basic trust in the creative power that sustains the life even of
the birds of the air and the grass and lilies of the field. Such
anxiety feeds on the ignorance of the source of true life and
compels one to attempt to secure life by amassing wealth or
collecting things (Matt. 6:25–33). It is enough for the disciple to

pray, "Give us this day our daily bread" (Matt. 6:11); for that
source of life that nourishes flora and fauna will provide especially for man's needs. The feeding of the five thousand was a
display of charity demonstrating that while man lives by bread,
he does not live by bread alone (Mark 6:34; Matt. 4:3; Luke 4:4;
John 6:35). The poor who would participate in the kingdom
must, as Jesus—himself a poor man—be merciful as God is merciful.

Theology of Reversal

The apocalyptic thrust of Jesus' message is seen in his teaching that the kingdom would be accompanied by a reversal of
the existing social order.[19] The respected in society would reject and in turn be excluded from the kingdom, while the poor
and sinners would be admitted into membership. The apocalyptic theology of reversal carried with it the understanding
that the economic structure would be subjected to reform, to
be brought about by God's power. The ministry of Jesus itself
was a sign of this turning of the tables, when the poor would be
privileged and the rich excluded.

This theology of reversal is especially apparent in Luke, but
is present in the other synoptic Gospels as well. Many would
come from east and west, north and south, to sit down at the
table in the Kingdom of God, there to dine with Abraham,
Isaac, Jacob, and all the prophets; while those Jews who were
heirs of this heritage would be thrust out (Luke 13:26–30; Matt.
8:11–12). The inversion produced by the kingdom would be like
a man who gave a great banquet for his son; when the invited
guests excused themselves the man instructed his servant, "Go
out quickly to the streets and lanes of the city, and bring in the
poor and maimed and blind and lame" (Luke 14:21). The servant
compelled the common people to come in off the streets, to fill
the hall, and to consume the fare that the original guests would
not be allowed to taste (Luke 14:16–24; Matt. 22:1–10). The king-

dom also could be compared to the prodigal son who returned home penniless after wasting his inheritance. Mumbling as he came up the road, "Father, I have sinned against heaven and before you; I am no longer worthy to be called your son," he fell into the arms of a loving father who joyfully celebrated his return with gifts of shoes, a robe, and a ring. The fatted calf was butchered for the merry feast of reconciliation. But the elder brother who had always stayed at home, having learned the meaning of the music and dancing, stood angrily outside and refused to enter (Luke 15:11–32).

The apocalyptic theme of economic reversal is vividly portrayed in the parable of the rich man, Dives, and Lazarus (Luke 16:19–31). Dives enjoyed his luxuries and daily partook of his culinary delights, while at his gate the poor and sick Lazarus craved—along with the dogs that licked his sores—the crumbs that fell from the rich man's table. Both men died. Then Dives, tormented in the Hadean flames, looked up to see Lazarus in the paradisiac comfort of Abraham's bosom. The tormented's plea for a single drop of water to cool his tongue was refused. Abraham replied, "Son, remember that you in your lifetime received your good things, and Lazarus in like manner evil things; but now he is comforted here, and you are in anguish" (Luke 16:25). There is no mention of the moral character of either man; Dives is not declared wicked or Lazarus virtuous. The one was rich and the other poor, but the time of reversal comes.[20]

The theology of reversal is found in many of Jesus' sayings about the first shall be last (Matt. 19:30; Mark 10:31; Luke 13:30); he who humbles himself will be exalted (Luke 14:11, 18:14); whoever attempts to save his life will lose it (Luke 17:33). Life in the kingdom would be the opposite of that expected: "Let the greatest among you become as the youngest, and the leader as one who serves" (Luke 22:26). Those who were least expected —like the Samaritan who cared for the half-dead Jew, beaten and robbed—would be representatives of the kingdom (Luke

10:29–37). Nowhere would the changing scene be more clearly observed than in the economic order. "Blessed are you poor, for yours is the kingdom of God. Blessed are you that hunger now, for you shall be satisfied" (Luke 6:20–21). This good news the poor heard proclaimed while the wealthy were warned: "But woe to you that are rich, for you have received your consolation. Woe to you that are full now, for you shall hunger" (Luke 6:24–25). The coming of the kingdom would bring in its wake a wave of economic revolution. Matthew tended to spiritualize these beatitudes by writing: "Blessed are the poor in spirit—" and "Blessed are those who hunger and thirst for righteousness —" (Matt. 5:3, 6). However, the text of Luke is considered closer to Jesus' intention.[21]

From Mark comes yet another provocative saying of Jesus concerning the economics of the kingdom (Mark 10:28–31; cf. Luke 18:28–30; Matt. 19:27–30). In response to Peter's statement that Jesus' disciples had left everything in order to follow him, Jesus replied that there was no one who had forfeited family or fortune "who will not receive a hundredfold now in this time, houses and brothers and sisters and mothers and children and lands, with persecutions, and in the age to come eternal life." The implications of such a promise were disconcerting even to the other synoptists, who both preferred to abbreviate this saying by omitting the specific items promised.[22]

The question may no longer be avoided: Did Jesus sanction a lower-class movement and advocate that the Kingdom of God would embrace an economic revolution? The answer is not simple and the nature of the Gospel tradition leads one to be cautious in attempting to reply. First, Jesus' ministry was directed primarily toward those rejected by society. These people received his message with joy because they were fully conscious of their dependent state and open to what the future might bring; they had everything to gain and little to lose.[23] The promise of a social transformation contributed to Jesus' initial popularity. Later many of this same group became disillusioned and perplexed at what the kingdom really was to be (cf. John 6:66; Mark 4:10–12). The rich, on the other hand, who trusted in their wealth and status, could only be disturbed by news of a coming economic reversal. If the conviction of economic revolution spread widely among the poor, they might attempt to realize their expectations through violence, as many Zealots advocated.

Jesus did call for economic change, but he did not trust in the government (Luke 13:32; John 19:10–11) or in the innate goodness of the human heart to bring about the transformation. His proclamation of the kingdom was apocalyptic in nature and his expectation of a social revolution was grounded in the sovereignty of God over all creation. Jesus did not expect the kingdom to arrive through man's efforts, either violent or benevolent. The kingdom would come when God's mercy was acknowledged and shared "on earth as it is in heaven." Hence compassion would redefine the nature of the economic order. To those men who trusted in their riches this understanding would provide little comfort, for it challenged them to make humanitarian deeds rather than profits the measure of a sound economy. Their obdurate possession of wealth in the face of their brother's suffering and misery was a rejection of divine mercy.

Jesus shared with the apocalyptists the conviction that the present age was influenced by demonic powers. However, in contrast to those visionaries who awaited a future cataclysmic destruction of the present order, Jesus proclaimed the present hour of God's action, which called for radical compassion toward one's fellows. While not rejecting the apocalyptic hope of an age to come, otherworldly visions did not distract him from human needs and social justice. Those who responded to his message of the kingdom expressed their joy quite naturally in the sharing of their selves and worldly possessions with one another. This community, formed by the acknowledgment of compassion as the presence of the divine, shared the spirit of

Jesus and expressed their charity through using their common
goods for the common welfare. It was like the family of God's
people in which each gained brothers and sisters, mothers and
fathers, lands and houses—a hundredfold.

Give Alms

The new economic order required the management of
wealth for humanitarian service. "Sell your possessions, and
give alms; provide yourselves with purses that do not grow old,
with a treasure in the heavens that does not fail, where no thief
approaches and no moth destroys. For where your treasure is,
there will your heart be also" (Luke 12:33–34; Matt. 6:19–21). It
was such a demand that turned the rich young man sorrowfully
away from the kingdom (Matt. 19:21–22; Mark 10:21–22; Luke
18:22–23) and yet, when accepted by Zacchaeus, brought salvation to his house (Luke 19:8–10). Jesus and his disciples gave alms
to the poor from their money box, the treasury administered by
Judas from which their common needs were supplied. These
alms were bestowed especially at feast times (John 12:6, 13:29).[24]

The givings of alms began with the surrender of one's life to
that power of life evident all about one. Jesus taught that one
whose life was secured by material possessions could never
overcome his anxieties and be free from the tyranny of things.
"But give for alms those things which are within; and behold,
everything is clean for you" (Luke 11:41). True holiness was the
acceptance of love as the final meaning of life; possessions could
then be used compassionately. The new economic order
emerged as God's mercy became sovereign over the management of possessions. "Give to every one who begs from you; and
of him who takes away your goods, do not ask them again. And
as you wish that men would do to you, do so to them" (Luke
6:30–31; Matt. 5:42). The so-called "golden rule" is stated in the
context of sharing material possessions. "But love your enemies,
and do good, and lend, expecting nothing in return; and your

reward will be great, and you will be sons of the Most High; for he is kind to the ungrateful and the selfish. Be merciful, even as your Father is merciful" (Luke 6:35–36). Jesus encouraged his followers to invite to a banquet not those who would be prepared to reciprocate, but the poor, maimed, lame, and blind who could not repay. The disciples could look to the resurrection, when the just would be recompensed (Luke 14:12–14). If a disciple were sued in court and his cloak taken away, he should give to the plaintiff his coat as well and demonstrate to him the difference between compulsion and compassion (Luke 6:29; Matt. 5:40).

While the giving of alms should be prompted by genuine concern, the payment of tithes or contributions could not substitute for mercy and justice. Jesus criticized some of the Pharisees for being meticulous in tithing of mint, dill, and cumin, the lesser-used spices, while neglecting the weightier considerations of the law such as justice, mercy, and faith (Luke 11:42; Matt. 23:23).[25] Philanthropic gifts were often given with public display in order to win prestige (Matt. 6:2–4). True acts of charity were to be performed in that secrecy that only God sees and rewards.

Personal relations took precedence over religious giving and ritual sacrifices. If one were offering his gift at the altar and recalled that he was alienated from his fellow, he should first seek reconciliation. Then he may offer his sacrifice. True worship of God was inextricably bound up with love and forgiveness of one's fellow man (Matt. 5:23–26, 6:14–15). Especially did the needs of one's parents take precedence over religious offerings. Jesus censured the Pharisees and scribes for sanctioning the practice of some Jews who dedicated to God money that was needed to provide for their parents (Mark 7:9–13; Matt. 15:1–9).[26]

The sphere of one's responsibility was not limited to family, neighborhood, or nation; it was wherever need was found. From the lawyer who recognized that the greatest commandment was "You shall love the Lord your God with all your heart, and with all your soul, and with all your strength, and with all your mind; and your neighbor as yourself" (Luke 10:27), the question came, "And who is my neighbor?" Jesus answered with the parable about a Jew who was robbed, stripped, beaten, and left half dead. The victim was passed by a priest and a Levite before a Samaritan, a member of a despised nation, ministered to him. Then Jesus asked the lawyer, who proved to be a neighbor to the man robbed, his own question. He replied, "The one who showed mercy on him." Jesus then said, "Go and do likewise." The lawyer, in order to determine the outer limits of that community in which love and care might properly be expected, had asked: "Who is my neighbor?" But Jesus pointed out that the lawyer should be a merciful neighbor to any man in need.[27]

The size and character of the gift that concern prompts was to be appropriate to the needs of the one and proportionate to the ability of the other (Luke 12:48). But even so slight a gift as a cup of cold water would not go unrewarded. Two copper coins placed in the treasury by an impoverished widow were valued as a richer gift than much larger sums contributed routinely by the affluent (Mark 12:41–44; Luke 21:1–4). Even the poor could have mercy.[28]

Jesus' message of the dawning kingdom, with the new economy altering the regulation of goods, was not oblivious to the present forces controlling the political and economic life of the Jews. When confronted with the question of whether to pay the taxes levied by Rome, he requested a coin and asked whose image it bore (Mark 12:13–17; Matt. 22:15–22; Luke 20:20–26). "Caesar's," was the answer. And Jesus replied, "Render to Caesar the things that are Caesar's, and to God the things that are God's."[29]

The Gospels also express a word of caution to those who would make the poor themselves and not mercy the measure of life in the kingdom. While Jesus sat at the table in Simon the leper's home, a woman came and anointed his head with a very expensive ointment (Mark 14:3–9; Matt. 26: 6–13). When some indignant onlookers raised the complaint that the ointment might better have been sold for a considerable sum and the proceeds distributed to the poor, Jesus defended his benefactress. He remarked that "You always have the poor with you, and whenever you will, you can do good to them."[30] A similar warning against letting the kingdom be understood as simply a welfare program is implicit in the Johannine account of the feeding of the five thousand. Following this sign—told similarly to the presentation in the synpotic Gospels, where Jesus fed the multitude by multiplying five barley loaves and two fish—some of those fed sought out Jesus again. To them he said, "Truly, truly, I say to you, you seek me, not because you saw signs, but because you ate your fill of the loaves. Do not labor for the food which perishes, but for the food which endures to eternal life —" (John 6:26–27).[31] The true bread is not physical, but is the compassion that prompted Jesus to care for the hungry. John made it clear that the power of eternal life was the power of Love.

The presupposition of Jesus' message of the kingdom was the conviction that the power sustaining all life is benevolent and merciful. Trusting in this power, one might free himself from the anxiety that results from securing life by multiplying things. One could then be free to respond to the needs of his fellow man knowing that his actions were acceptable to God. If evil men could on occasion make a fitting response to another's need, how much more would the Father sustain those whose life was grounded in him with that love that the kingdom would bring (Luke 11:9–13; Matt. 7:7–11).

III

Poverty Programs in the Early Church

1. The Beginnings of Christianity

Jesus was crucified outside the walls of Jerusalem under the ambiguous title "King of the Jews." Both the Jewish and Roman officials detected the incipient threat to the status quo implicit in his life and teachings. But the Cross did not destroy the spirit of compassion that he had expressed and the hope for the coming kingdom that he had aroused. The first disciples in Jerusalem tried to put into practice a concern for the weak and poor, a concern they had witnessed in Jesus. They enacted an aggressive program of benevolence and created a revolution in their own economic practices.

The Kerygma

The Book of Acts indicates that the poverty program among the Jersualem Christians grew directly from the message, or kerygma, that they proclaimed.[1] They believed they were on the threshold of a new age that required taking seriously the fellowship of love. The messianic age had dawned with the ministry of Jesus, culminating in his death and Resurrection. The risen Lord had been exalted by God to sit at his right hand in glory, from whence Christ had sent the Holy Spirit into the church as a sign of his present power. Shortly, however, Christ would return and the messianic age would be consummated—at the parousia. It was this experience of salvation—the freedom from sin and the hope for an early return of Christ—that enabled the early church to take radical measures in regulating its economy.

The Setting of Luke-Acts

Before investigating the nature of the Jerusalem Christians' program to provide for their own poor, it may prove helpful to notice the historical setting of Acts. Available information points to Rome as the place of composition for the two-volume work Luke-Acts.[2] Luke probably composed the Book of Acts during the mid-eighties, looking back across half a century to describe the origin of Christianity and the apostolic community. The church in Rome was founded only a brief period after the beginning of Christianity, perhaps by some who were in Jerusalem when Peter preached the first Christian sermon. Acts states that among those who had come to Jerusalem to celebrate the feast of Pentecost were "visitors from Rome, both Jews and proselytes" (Acts 2:10); these may have returned to Rome with the kerygma. In any event, when Paul wrote to the Roman church in the mid-fifties he addressed a vigorous congregation whose faith was proclaimed in all the world (Rom. 1:8). Christianity grew rapidly in Rome, initially within the Jewish colony there and later among the Gentiles.

Accompanying the numerical growth of the church was an increasing suspicion and hatred of Christians among the Roman populace, who were disturbed by this strange religion from the East. The emperor Nero (A.D. 54–68) capitalized on this widespread prejudice by blaming the great fire in Rome on the Christians, thereby diverting attention from himself and the report that he had ordered the fire set. Nero could thus vindi-

cate himself as well as vent his own sadism.[3] He heaped upon
the Christians atrocities that were the refinements of a per-
verted mind, and a large number of them were arrested and
martyred. Some were dressed in the skins of wild animals and
then torn to death by dogs; others were crucified or burned at
the stake to illuminate Nero's garden parties at night.

The Roman historian Tacitus wrote that so great was the
suffering of the Christians that there arose a pity for them, and
the impression grew that they were being sacrificed because of
the ferocity of Nero, not for the good of the state. These extreme forms of punishment were reserved for the lower class
of people who had few rights and little standing in Rome. There
is a strong tradition that both Peter and Paul died in the
Neronian persecution, which began in A.D. 64.[4] Two decades
later Luke wrote Acts at a time when Christians were still
suspect in Rome and the church was comprised largely of people from the lower class, i.e., slaves and poor freemen. He wrote
motivated in part by the desire to present to his Roman readers
an apology for the Christian faith.

Luke's View of Christianity in Jerusalem

The source of Luke's information concerning the Jerusalem
church and its benevolence policy is not certain. However
there was a considerable amount of travel between Jerusalem
and Rome and knowledge may have been obtained from several sources, even from Paul and Peter. There is a marked
similarity between the narrative of Acts 2:1–47 and 5:17–24 and
that of Acts 3:1–5:16. This parallelism raises three questions: Is
Luke repeating himself by giving two accounts of the same
events? Are the events described actually two separate but
similar occurrences? Or are there two separate traditions of the
same events that came down to Luke and that he tried to
combine into a unified narrative? Regardless of the correct
answer, the doublet in which the life of the early church is

summarized (Acts 2:42–47 and 4:31–35) should be studied to-gether.[5]

Luke depicted a somewhat idealized picture of the life of the Jerusalem Christians. He saw it as a time of great enthusiasm because the Holy Spirit filled the community and manifested its presence in various ways. There was a sense of awe arising from the conviction that God had acted in the death and Resurrection of Jesus to usher in a new day of human history. Excitement sprang from the expectation that the parousia would fulfill the promise of the messianic age. Great power and grace produced a bold way of life characterized by joy and generosity. Celebration of the new life was typified by wholehearted devotion and single-minded commitment to Jesus and the hope grounded in him. Signs and wonders were performed by the apostles, who provided leadership for the community of the faithful.

2. Care of the Poor

The unity of faith found its natural expression in the sharing of possessions. These first Christians exemplified their loyalty to Jesus not only by living in the spirit of his life but also by continuing the sharing of material resources that he and his followers had practiced. The term "fellowship" *(koinonia)* was not limited to the meaning of social exchange or similarity of religious belief; it meant a sharing of life that extended to one's possessions. Love for a brother required that his need take precedence over the right of private ownership. The purpose of these Christians was not to form a communistic group per se. They wanted to respond to their brothers' need with a compassion consistent with the character of Jesus and appropriate to the new age. Not to share all of life would be a betrayal of the former and a denial of the latter. The Letter of James, which an unlikely tradition ascribes to James the brother of Jesus and leader of the Jerusalem church, does reflect a definite Jewish background and may be noted to advantage.[6] The author of James was concerned about the affirmation of faith and good will that did not also find expression in specific acts of care. He pointed out that if a brother or sister were hungry and shabby, simply wishing him or her well saying, "Go in peace, be warmed and filled," was not an act of faith unless those things needed for the body were also provided. "So faith by itself, if it has no works, is dead" (James 2:14–17).

Table Fellowship

Table fellowship was a testimony of the disciples' common life and the breaking of bread together a sign of the communion of love. Among the first Christians there was no sharp distinction drawn between the meals that they shared in their fellowship of love and the Lord's Supper.[7] Luke suggested the close connection between the two when he stated that "day by day, attending the temple together and breaking bread in their homes, they partook of food with glad and generous hearts" (Acts 2:46). That the breaking of bread was essentially a religious act is demonstrated by its association with the disciples devoting themselves to the apostles' teaching and fellowship and prayer (2:42). Paul used the word *koinonia* in writing about the fellowship with Christ that is present in the Lord's Supper. "The cup of blessing which we bless, is it not a participation [κοινωνία] in the blood of Christ? The bread which we break, is it not a participation [κοινωνία] in the body of Christ?" (1 Cor. 10:16). The communion with Christ and fellowship with one another within his body, the church, was appropriately expressed in the festivity of meals shared in the spirit of love and brotherhood.

Celebration of the new age was a daily event. The Eucharist itself had been instituted following the Passover meal. The first Christians considered every occasion of fellowship an act of worship. It is probable that many of the poor in the Jerusalem church found in these meals their primary means of subsistence. These love feasts combined the elements of worship and fellowship with the practical concern of nourishing the poor. The practice of celebrating the Lord's Supper in conjunction with the agape feast was widespread in the early church, though later the two became separated.

Paul discouraged the Corinthians from continuing to use their assemblies as church suppers, because they were perverting the purpose of fellowship.[8] The divisions within the church became obvious when they would not wait for one another in order to eat together. One would have excess and become intoxicated; another would go home hungry. It was not what they ate and drank that concerned Paul, but he was offended by the embarrassment and humiliation of those who had nothing. To eat one's fill in the presence of a hungry brother and not share with him was a denial of that love the meal was meant to celebrate. In another context Paul stressed that "the kingdom of God does not mean food and drink but righteousness and peace and joy in the Holy Spirit" (Rom. 14:17). He who eats the bread and drinks the cup of the communion and does not discern the body of Christ, i.e., that community formed and sustained by the power of his love, "eats and drinks judgment upon himself" (1 Cor. 11:29).

Jews and Christians felt that eating together was a sign of acceptance and affection. In the early church, table fellowship both grew out of and witnessed to the common faith that the Christians shared. Dietary regulations tended to disappear in the Christian community in the realization that thankfulness to God and love for each other constituted the true holiness of their meals (Acts 15:20, 29, 21:25; Rom. 14:1–23; 1 Cor. 8:1–13). To refuse to eat with a Christian brother was inexcusable for it made some standard other than the one faith in Jesus as Lord the test of fellowship. At Antioch Paul opposed Peter because when certain Jews came from James in Jerusalem, Peter in fear no longer ate with the Gentile Christians (Gal. 2:11–16). To segregate the Christian community through adopting external values, whether cultural or religious, could only result in destructive divisions within the body of Christ (cf. 1 Cor. 1:10, 3:1–8). On the other hand, a brother who rejected the faith by which the community was formed and sustained should be excluded from the table fellowship as an overt sign of his denial of the faith (1 Cor. 5:3–5, 9–13). To be ostracized from the fellowship and agape feasts was a severe disciplinary act intended to make the apostate aware of his condition and to draw him back into the community of the faithful.

Community of Goods

A program to provide for the poor in the Christian community spontaneously arose as concern for a brother's or sister's need led to deeds of love. Compassion for a fellow Christian, not the implementation of an economic theory, motivated the giving. Christians with possessions and goods, such as real estate and personal property, sold them and brought the proceeds to the apostles for distribution to the poor (Acts 2:45, 4:34–35). Their selling of lands was a testimony to the new understanding of the Kingdom of God. Land had been promised by God to his people; each family had been concerned to protect its heritage in the Promised Land. But now lands were sold in the realization that the Kingdom of God was a community in which his spirit dwelt. The imperfect tense of the Greek verb "to sell" *(piprasko)* indicates that possessions were sold over an extended period of time rather than all at once. This liquidation of assets was regulated by the particular needs and the private decision of the contributor.[9]

When Acts generalizes that "all who believed were together and had all things in common" (2:44), it is not likely that all the property of every Christian was sold and the money placed in a general fund from which the needs of all were met. Rather, the context indicates that the property of each Christian was

used in the best interest of the community as a whole.[10] Those
who had homes opened them for worship and fellowship meals
(Acts 2:46; cf. 12:12), hence private possessions were no longer
used for personal comforts. As new converts were made their
goods might also be contributed for the relief of poverty. As
already noted, how much property should be sold and when it
should be marketed was determined privately by the owner.
The church did not reject the right of private ownership. Contributions were motivated by a voluntary willingness to sacrifice
personal holdings for the welfare of the less fortunate. Barnabas
is held up as an example of those who freely chose to act in order
to supply the need (Acts 4:36–37). This specific mention not
only introduces Barnabas for the role he plays later in Acts, but
also by singling out his generosity it indicates that not everyone
had done the same.

The incident regarding Ananias and Sapphira (Acts 5:1–11)
bears out the right of private ownership and the lack of compulsion that characterized the community's philanthropy. This
couple, impressed by the sacrifice of those who sold possessions
and donated all the proceeds, sold a piece of property and
colluded to contribute a part of what they received while claiming that they, too, were giving all. When the deception was
detected by Peter, he affirmed that they were under no obligation to sell, and having sold, they were at liberty to use the funds
as they pleased. However, since they had lied, their prevarica-
tion was an offense against the Holy Spirit and a violation of the
nature of the community. Acts states that at Peter's rebuke both
Ananias and Sapphira in turn fell down and died.[11]

The experience of togetherness and unity of faith resulted
ideally in the breaking down of social and economic distinctions
within the community. This equality was not because each possessed an equal amount of goods but because all were brethren
in the body of Christ. The writer of James advised that no
partiality should be permitted to disrupt the egalitarian status
within the church (James 2:1–7). If one man entered the assem-

bly wearing gold rings and fine clothes and another came in shabbily dressed, both should be given an equally warm welcome. No discrimination should be expressed by seating arrangements. After all, the writer reminded his readers, who appear to be primarily from the poorer class, it is the rich who so often oppress you and the poor who are chosen to be rich in faith and heirs of the Kingdom of God (James 2:5–6; cf. 5:1–6).

In addition to the meals served daily in the homes of Christians there was a daily distribution of money to provide for immediate needs and to prevent unnecessary deprivation. These funds were allocated by the apostles from the monies contributed for this purpose. There was great emphasis placed upon honesty and integrity in matters dealing with the poverty funds. Acts states that those who gave from their own resources laid the money "at the apostles' feet," which indicates a legal custom demonstrating the relinquishing of right of ownership.[12] There were many people in the community who might expect assistance. The apostles themselves were probably supported by the church, since after leaving Galilee and coming to Jerusalem they would have given up their means of livelihood. Some Jews who came to Jerusalem to celebrate the feast of Pentecost and then became Christians may have postponed their return to their homelands or decided to stay permanently until the parousia, which they believed to be near. These people would have soon exhausted their travel funds and needed help. Others who would receive relief were the sick and disabled, the aged, the widows and orphans, victims of some disaster, and those Christians who were imprisoned.[13]

3. Social Causes of Rapid Growth

A large segment of the Jerusalem church was comprised of the poor. Acts clearly indicates that the church initially experienced a rapid growth; the three thousand souls who be-

lieved on the day of Pentecost soon increased to five thousand
men alone as day by day the Lord added to their number (Acts
2:41, 47, 4:4, 6:7). While the actual count is subject to question,
the report of phenomenal growth appears to be reliable. No
doubt the kerygma itself—the message of salvation that the
apostles proclaimed—produced extraordinary results, a point
often made by New Testament scholars. It should be kept in
mind that there were also significant sociological forces that
contributed to this numerical growth. The kerygma provided
the new self-understanding for the community, which then
acted consistently with the faith which it embraced. The program to care for human need was a proclamation itself of the
meaning of life. How better could one testify to the character
of the new age, the love for his brother, the nearness of the
return of Christ than to sell his possessions and give the money
for the poor? The integrity between proclamation and use of
possessions did not go unnoticed. Many were influenced by the
new life emerging within the Christian community.

Because Jerusalem was the center of Judaism, the Holy City
in which the temple worship was observed, it attracted pilgrims
from many distant lands. Much of the economy of Jerusalem
was based on the trade resulting from these visitors. They were
disposed to be especially generous with beggars, since alms
given in the Holy City at holy times were considered especially
meritorious. This generosity drew numerous beggars—indi-
gents, the weak, and fakes—who exploited the benevolence of
the pious. Jerusalem also housed a disproportionately large
number of elderly who came to die in the Holy City or perhaps
to await the coming messiah (Luke 2:25, 36). To these were
added the scholars who, while respected for their knowledge
and their wisdom, were not paid for their teaching.[14]

Measures were taken by the leaders in Jerusalem to provide
for the needs of the poor in the church. The spirit of concern,
the enthusiasm of the fellowship, and the deeds of charity had
their effect on the resident Jews, prompting many of the lower

class to join the Christian community. Their number increased so rapidly and the burden of caring for them became so great that new policies had to be instituted both to obtain more funds and to distribute them more equitably.

4. Special Concern for Widows

The Hellenistic Widows

A special problem for the church was presented by the widows, many of whom lived in Jerusalem. In addition to those who were natives of the city, there were widows from foreign lands who had been drawn to the Holy City by their piety and expectation of charity. Those Jews whose permanent residence was outside Palestine, that is, in the Diaspora, are designated in Acts as the Hellenists, or Greek-speaking Jews, in contrast to the Hebrews, or Hebrew (Aramaic)-speaking Jerusalemites.[15] The complaint arose from the Christian Hellenists that their widows were being neglected in the daily distribution of relief (Acts 6:1–6). This discrimination resulted from considering citizens of Jerusalem to have priority over foreign Christian Jews and it may well have seemed appropriate to some, since the funds were being provided by local Jewish Christians.

The apostles were responsible for the welfare program. They, too, were probably supported by the church and the charge of discrimination raised the delicate question of conflict of interest. Therefore the issue arose as to what should be the apostles' primary sphere of responsibility and attention: the ministry of the word or the welfare program. The apostles agreed that it would not be fitting for them to "give up preaching the word of God to serve tables" (Acts 6:2). The program of caring for the poor had arisen inevitably from the nature of the community's fellowship and the material needs of some of its members. However, the kerygma was the formative power of the church and, while it should lead to charity, it should not be replaced by social action.

The apostles devised a plan for the Hellenists themselves to select seven men from their own number to be in charge of the distribution to their widows. These were to be responsible men of integrity, highly esteemed, and full of the Holy Spirit. The names of the seven elected for this service indicate that they were all Hellenists: Stephen, Philip, Prochorus, Nicanor, Timon, Parmenas, and Nicolaus. They were appointed for this ministry by the laying on of the apostles' hands and with prayer.[16] This expansion in the organization and administration of the poverty program alleviated the immediate difficulty but did not solve the problem of caring for the widows in the early church.

The Widows at Corinth

The care for widows continued to be a major concern for the Christian community as it spread beyond Jerusalem. The proper disposition toward widows was a question for the Corinthian church, and they asked Paul what course of action would be advisable regarding both widows and others who were unmarried. Paul's advice was that it was well for them to remain single as he did (1 Cor. 7:8). He supported this judgment by reference to the "impending distress" that he believed was imminent. Paul anticipated a time in the not-too-distant future when the church would be subjected to tribulations—those apocalyptic disruptions preceding the full arrival of the kingdom—and he wanted to spare the Christians the additional anxiety caused by concern for a husband or wife (1 Cor. 7:25–26). Paul was further convinced that a single person could more readily give undivided loyalty and service to Jesus as Lord if unhindered by family responsibilities (1 Cor. 7:32–38). While permitting marriage, Paul considered it a less acceptable course at that time and a concession to physical passions (1 Cor. 7:9).

This is the clearest example in the New Testament of an interim ethic, i.e., an ethical teaching controlled by the belief in the imminence of the parousia. But since the interim proved to be longer than Paul anticipated, his advice contributed to the seriousness of an already difficult problem. [17]

The Order of Widows

It is impossible to say how widely Paul's advice was circulated and how many people took it seriously. However, the First Letter of Paul to Timothy, a book composed in the first half of the second century, reveals the efforts to reduce the number of widows supported by the church (1 Tim. 5:3–16).[18] It reflects a situation in which the number of widows cared for by the church had increased to the point that measures had to be taken to reduce the financial burden. Some of the younger widows were idlers and busybodies, gadding about from house to house and gossiping. They had "strayed after Satan," and their impropriety and immorality were creating criticisms of the church from their non-Christian neighbors. The stipulations for receiving support from the church were made more stringent. Paul's advice that the widows should remain single was reversed. Younger widows were encouraged to marry, have children, and be homemakers. This policy helped to solve the problems of immorality and idleness as well as lack of support.

Another policy aimed at reducing the number of widows on the church roll insisted that the woman's family assume the responsibility for her support. It stressed the point that it was a religious obligation for the children to provide for their aging mothers and grandmothers. "If any one does not provide for his relatives, and especially for his own family, he has disowned the faith and is worse than an unbeliever" (1 Tim. 5:8). If, however, a widow were without any family, she could receive a livelihood from the church provided she met certain qualifications.

She must be a woman of at least sixty years who had been the

wife of one husband and brought up children. She must have
the reputation of being a person devoted to prayer and good
deeds and not reluctant to perform kind if perhaps unpleasant
acts of service to those in need. Specifically, she should have
"shown hospitality, washed the feet of the saints, [and] relieved
the afflicted" (1 Tim. 5:10). It would be expected that she also
assist the community by instructing the younger women concerning family relationships, child rearing, and domestic arts
(Titus 2:3–5; cf. 1 Tim. 2:9–12).

The widows who qualified for the church rolls comprised a
special group within the community and also functioned somewhat like practical nurses in ministering to the needs of the sick
and infirm. They were encouraged to continue the generous
way of life for which they were already appreciated. These
widows pledged themselves to the service of the community
and vowed not to remarry but to dedicate themselves wholly
to Christ and his service.[19] They formed an order that supplemented the work of the elders and deacons in regulating and
caring for the needs of the community. Thus the church attempted to transform what had been a liability into an asset by
supporting those widows who in turn ministered to the needs
of the saints. This policy not only gave these women a useful
function and a means of support but also provided them with
the opportunity to demonstrate the love that Jesus revealed.

5. The Dole at Rome

When Luke wrote the Book of Acts in Rome, he may well
have reflected upon the sharp contrast between the Roman
welfare programs, calculated primarily to pacify the mob, and
the charity of the Jerusalem Christians, motivated by faith in
Jesus as the Christ and love for their brethren. Rome contained
a large number of rabble, many of whom were attracted to the
city by the regular and frequent distributions of relief. Granting

provisions for the poor citizens of Rome had an ancient tradition extending back at least to the time of the Republic when the Gracchi, Tiberius and Gaius, championed the cause of the poor masses. During the brief period that Gaius was tribune, before his assassination in 121 B.C., he instituted a program of government-subsidized grain in order to make cheap grain available for the proletariat. Subsequent rulers continued to grapple with the problems created by the poor. Julius Caesar, after returning to Rome in 46 B.C., reduced the number of citizens on the dole from 320,000 to 150,000, developing extensive public works projects in order to make work for the poor and unemployed. By the time Augustus (31 B.C.–A.D. 14) became princeps of Rome the number of poor had risen sharply, and as a much-needed economy measure, he cut those eligible for the dole from 320,000 to 200,000.[20]

The Roman mobs took the dole for granted and no emperor could ignore its effectiveness in pacifying the people. Nero, especially, used the dole as a means of manipulating public opinion and winning popular support. The Roman historian Suetonius wrote that Nero missed no opportunity to display acts of public generosity. On one occasion, in addition to special favors for some of the high-ranking citizens, Nero granted 400 sesterces to each man in Rome.[21] Daily he had thrown to the people all kinds of presents: "these included a thousand birds of every kind each day, various kinds of food, tickets for grain, clothing, gold, silver, precious stones, pearls, paintings, slaves, beasts of burden, and even trained wild animals."[22] To some favorites he gave ships, blocks of houses, and farms. Nero also provided elaborate entertainment to placate the people: chariot races, stage plays, and gladiatorial shows. In the arena criminals were compelled to fight wild beasts and Christians were subjected to the greatest cruelties. Mock naval battles were fought and obscene shows performed. These spectaculars satisfied the populace's demand for sex and violence.[23] In keeping with this policy Vespasian (A.D. 69–79), the first of the

Flavian emperors, began the construction of the Flavian Am-
phitheater, or Colosseum, as it later came to be called. A decade
later, in A.D. 80, his son Titus (A.D. 79–81) dedicated the Colosseum just prior to the time that Luke wrote Acts.[24]

The dole in Rome became expected as a right of the citizens
and gradually made more and more people dependent on the
state. This fact did not go unnoticed by some of the critics of
Roman society. In his *Satire*, written in the first third of the
second century, Juvenal lampooned the Roman citizens for
standing in line to receive the dole and attempting to obtain
more than their share by various ingenious but fraudulent
tricks. He decried the apathy of the mob of Remus: "the people
that once bestowed commands, consulships, legions and all else
now meddles no more and longs eagerly for just two things—
Bread and Games" *(panem et circenses).*[25]

Luke was a writer who was sensitive to Roman policy while
living within a Christian community comprised largely of members of the lower classes. He could not easily avoid being aware
of the contrast between the welfare policies of the Roman state
and the care for the poor in the Jerusalem church. The former
he could observe at first hand; the latter he knew from reports
that he tended to idealize, although he did not ignore the problems encountered by the Jerusalem Christians. It is helpful to
distinguish between the two different spirits at work in Rome
and Jerusalem.

The evolution of Rome into a welfare state was accompanied
by a greater dependence of the people on the government.[26]
During the period of the Republic, Roman life sustained the
ideals of democratic government and individual initiative. The
people continuously resisted the government's attempts to
solve problems that they believed the individual could handle
better. Social legislation did not gain momentum until the period of the Empire, when democratic rule gave way to autocra-
tic government. This paternalistic government resulted in part
from the infiltration into Rome of foreigners and slaves who did

not share the democratic values of the Republic. Rome's social legislation was not devoid of humanitarian interests, but in the hands of the emperors, who were under pressure to administer the vast empire, the dole became an effective tool for pacifying the masses and preserving the *pax Romana*. Even those emperors who questioned the wisdom of the dole were reluctant to end it because of the ensuing unrest and riots that were certain to occur.

On the other hand, the relief program of the Jerusalem Christians was not simply a pragmatic solution to the problems of poverty but a kerygmatic expression of their new life in Christ. It was an overt testimony to their discovery of the humanity-in-community created by the Christ event. Economic disparity was experienced as a violation of their fellowship as members of the body of Christ. Their deeds of ministering to their poor were a concrete acknowledgement of their interdependence rather than of the dependence of one class upon another. The poverty program did not depersonalize or humiliate the recipient; it affirmed his identity as a member of the community whose worth was seen in terms of the measure of his faith, that common faith in Jesus that called the community into being. The Christians' humanitarian concern for their brother's need sprang from apocalyptic enthusiasm that prompted them to use their material goods as an opportunity to express that love that would be sovereign in the dawning new age.

The massive expense of the Roman welfare program was paid by consistently raising taxes, which placed an increasing burden on an economy already weakened by dwindling foreign markets and military expenditures. Taxes were exacted by compulsion as fiscal problems, especially inflation, were met with greater governmental control. Coinage was devalued; wages and prices were frozen; and finally, during the fourth century, the reforms of Constantine forced men and even their children to remain in their occupations. This regimentation of society stood in sharp contrast to the spirit of freedom characteristic of the Christian community, where contributions for the poor were given voluntarily as need, ability, and individual generosity dictated.

The dole was distributed without regard for moral reform and the corrupt aspects of Roman life remained unchanged. At most it was hoped that the recipient would take a job on one of the public works projects or settle in one of the colonies to help protect the frontier, and welfare was regulated in order to achieve these ends. In the early church, however, charity was not determined by moral worth because the community itself was predicated on the experience of grace and the acceptance of sinners. Neither was assistance granted as an enticement or incentive for one's becoming respectable. Rather, the Christian's morality was grounded in the experience of grace, where forgiveness and acceptance were expressions of divine love. They believed that this love was victorious in the life and death of Jesus and called them to share the same quality of life with one another.

The "mob of Remus" was not content to live by bread alone but demanded the games as a continual distraction from an otherwise miserable and often meaningless existence. The emperors supplied their demand with spectacles that were the extreme in entertainment. But the escape afforded by the games provided the spectator little meaning or hope for the future. The first Christians, too, were not content to live by bread alone. They shared their bread as an expression of the nature of the messianic community in which they lived. They celebrated life daily in meals served in their homes where their immediate joy of fellowship was enriched by the hope of the parousia.

6. Communism at Qumran

The poverty program of the Jerusalem Christians can be more clearly understood by comparison with the contemporary communistic group of Essenes settled at Qumran. The discovery of the Dead Sea Scrolls twenty-five years ago has vastly enlarged our information concerning the Essenes, who were known previously from the writings of the first-century Jewish historian, Josephus, and his younger contemporary, Philo, the Alexandrian Jewish philosopher-apologist. Well over a century before the beginning of Christianity a devout group of Jews withdrew from Jerusalem in protest against the increasing Hellenization by the Hasmonean rulers and their claims to the priesthood. These Essenes established themselves in various locales; however, the best-known community was that founded at Khirbet Qumran, on the plateau overlooking the northwest shore of the Dead Sea. While this sect was never large in numbers, perhaps no more than four thousand, their quality of life, theology, and organization affords enlightening comparisons with the first Christians.

The Essenes' exodus from Jerusalem was provoked by a wicked priest who persecuted their leader and founder, whom they called the Teacher of Righteousness. They withdrew into the desolate desert region bordering on the Dead Sea in order to prepare for the coming messianic age. The Essenes anticipated a coming conflict in which the evil powers that frustrated their life would be destroyed. Following this great war, the reign of their two awaited messiahs would be inaugurated; one messiah would come from the royal house of David, the other from the priestly family of Aaron. Their existence was guided by this apocalyptic hope and life in the community was carefully regulated. The *Manual of Discipline,* or *Rule of the Community,* found in the caves at Qumran reveals the character of their life. The Essenes divided their time between work and worship, studying the Old Testament and meeting in general assembly morning and evening to pray. A strong sense of unity permeated their fellowship; they believed that the Holy Spirit guided their efforts to gain purity, obedience, and salvation. They lived with the conviction that they were the true heirs of Israel's heritage, hence the self-designation "Community of the New Covenant."

An elected central council composed of twelve laymen and three priests functioned as a judicial body.[27] The *Rule of the Community* stipulated punishments for infractions of required standards of conduct. Twice daily, at noon and in the evening, the Essenes assembled in the common dining hall for meals. While the food was simple, their sharing in table fellowship was an appropriate testimony to their common life. These meals held religious overtones that are apparent in the requirement that a priest must pronounce a prayer of blessing before the meal. Ten persons constituted a quorum.[28] In addition, these meals were probably eschatologically oriented. The daily repast was symbolic of the great messianic banquet in which the Essenes expected to share.

A result of the spirit of oneness and togetherness of the Qumran community was the practice of economic communism. The goods of the sect were kept in a common storehouse and were distributed by a supply officer as necessity dictated. To lie in matters concerning property was considered to be a most serious offense, since the economic well-being of the entire community depended on integrity regarding possessions. [29]

Admission to membership in the sect was closely regulated.[30] Every candidate had to be at least twenty years old and was examined publicly concerning his moral character and intellectual capacity as well as his motives for joining the sect. If he passed this examination, he was admitted to the first of two year-long probationary periods. During the first year he was not permitted to share in the common meals or in the resources of the community. If his conduct was approved after this novitiate, he was admitted to the community to serve the second year of probation. During this year all his property was held in escrow by an overseer, but he was not yet allowed to eat with the community or to draw on their common goods. If the second year was successfully completed, he then might be allowed full membership in the community by a general vote of the assembly and by taking an oath of allegiance. Then his own personal property was transferred to the common storehouse and he relinquished all rights of private ownership.

An exception to the strict practice of communism was made in the case of " 'specially holy men'—that is, of 'the men that walk blamelessly.' " The property of these presbyters was not put in the common pool because they were esteemed to be men of the highest integrity and above the temptations to which the less mature were subject.[31]

There are many interesting points of comparison between the Qumran community and the early church in Jerusalem. The similarities of emphasis on unity, possession of the Holy Spirit, apocalyptic orientation, messianic expectation, use of the Old Testament, fellowship meals, and sharing of goods all offer promise of better understanding of each religious community. However, there was a basic contrast in economic theory between the two groups. The Essenes practiced a strict communism by requiring their members to give up the right of private ownership. On the other hand, the early Christians recognized the right of private property but encouraged voluntary sharing for the common weal. Both groups found it advantageous to deposit their resources with designated officials for fairer distribution and both placed great stress on honesty in matters relating to property. While the Jerusalem Christians developed a poverty program to meet the needs of their poorer members, the communism practiced at Qumran made this type of program unnecessary.[32] The common meals at Qumran served twice daily with religious significance offers an interesting parallel to those Christians who daily broke bread in their homes with glad and generous hearts and partook of the Lord's Supper together.

The frugality and simplicity of life that characterized the Essenes' retreat to the desert in order to prepare a "highway for our God" were appropriately expressed in their designation

of themselves as the "Congregation of the Poor." The connota-
tion of this appellative was derived from the pious poor often
mentioned in the Psalms. While the word "poor" is mentioned
more often in Luke than in either of the other synoptic Gospels,
in Acts "poor" is not used at all, despite the attention given to
the poverty program in the Jerusalem church. It may well be
that Luke wished to avoid using a word for the Christian community that had connotations that would confuse his reader
because of its designation of the "pious poor" among the Jews
or Ebionites. Paul, however, spoke of the "poor among the
saints at Jerusalem" (Rom. 15:26; Gal. 2:10). But his usage seems
clearly to designate an economic rather than a spiritual condition.[33]

Parallels between the Essenes and the early Christians are
instructive not because one borrowed directly from the other
but rather because the two movements were siblings from the
same Jewish mother. Their responses to basic human problems
reflected their common cultural milieu while demonstrating
the originality of each group.[34]

The subsequent history of these two sects was largely determined by the Roman legions under the command of Titus.
Archaeology has revealed the grim fate of the Essenes at Qumran, whose settlement was devastated by the Romans in about
A.D. 68. The Essenes soon disappeared after this disaster. Just
prior to the siege of Titus and the destruction of Jerusalem in
A.D. 70, many of the Christians fled from Jerusalem; a number
of these refugees took up residence in the town of Pella across
the Jordan River.[35] After the razing of Jerusalem and the temple, the future of Christianity depended primarily on the Gentile churches, many of which were founded by Paul. However,
even before the destruction of Jerusalem, the poverty program
proved to be incapable of meeting the great demands placed on
it. The condition produced by the large numbers of poor attracted by the Gospel was complicated by famine (Acts 11:
27–30), and the leaders in the Jerusalem church sought addi-

tional sources of revenue. They turned to Paul, requesting that he collect funds among his Gentile mission congregations. The letters and ministry of Paul are interlaced with his efforts to raise these much-needed funds.

IV

Paul and the Collection

1. Remember the Poor

The efforts to care for the poor in the Jerusalem church were hindered by the famine that occurred between A.D. 46 and 48 during the reign of Claudius (A.D. 41–54).[1] Acts relates that prophets came to Antioch in Syria from Jerusalem, and one of them, Agabus, predicted that a great famine was imminent. To meet this crisis the church in Antioch resolved to send relief to their brethren in Jerusalem. This they did, sending it to the elders by Barnabas and Paul (Acts 11:27–30, 12:25). Paul's participation in taking this relief to Jerusalem may well have commended him for the larger collection that he was to undertake.[2]

The Significance of the Collection

In the Galatian letter Paul reviewed his relationship with the Jerusalem church and suggested how it happened that he should have been asked to raise funds for the poor there (Gal. 1:11–2:10). It is against this historical background that the significance of the collection for Paul must be understood. Paul's claim that he was eager to undertake this difficult task raises the question of his motivation for accepting this responsibility and the purpose that he considered the collection would serve. He had an obvious humanitarian concern to relieve the widespread physical suffering and deprivation among the Jerusalem Christians. However, Paul was motivated by other important reasons as well.

Before Paul had been converted to Christianity he had persecuted the church (Gal. 1:13, 23; 1 Cor. 15:9; Phil. 3:6; Acts 8:1–3). Immediately following his conversion in Damascus he went to Arabia; he then returned to Damascus before making his first visit to Jerusalem as a Christian, approximately three years after his conversion. He visited for fifteen days with Peter, but he saw none of the other apostles except James, the Lord's brother. After leaving Jerusalem he was still not well known among the churches in Judea. It was, however, reported among the Christians that " 'He who once persecuted us is now preaching the faith he once tried to destroy' " (Gal. 1:23). It was to Paul's advantage to minimize the opposition he had encountered in Jerusalem in relating his visit there.

But Acts states that there was considerable reservation in Jerusalem about accepting Paul into the Christian fellowship. Some were dubious about the sincerity of his conversion. It might well be, they thought, that Paul was attempting to infiltrate their membership in order to harass the community more effectively. The reticence of a number in the Jerusalem church to welcome Paul into full fellowship curtailed his ministry there. Acts further indicates that although Barnabas had attempted to vouch for Paul to the leaders in the church, Paul's ministry in Jerusalem was restricted primarily to the Greek-speaking Hellenists (Acts 9:26–30).

Paul's relationship with the mother church in Jerusalem was further strained by the fact that his missionary efforts were largely directed toward Gentiles. The fundamental question raised was whether a Gentile convert to Christianity was obligated to observe the Law of Moses, expecially the rite of circumcision. When a Jew in Jerusalem became a Christian, he accepted Jesus as the messiah but did not cease to observe those Jewish practices that were indigenous to his culture. Since Jews made no sharp distinction between civil laws and religious customs, practically it would have been impossible to abandon observance of the Mosaic law and traditions. Therefore, must a Gentile convert to Christianity living outside of Palestine be required to keep the Mosaic law? Paul's answer was no. A man is "justified by faith in Christ, and not by works of the law" (Gal. 2:16). He challenged his Gentile converts not to be enticed by those who would make the Law of Moses compulsory: "For freedom Christ has set us free; stand fast therefore, and do not submit again to a yoke of slavery" (Gal. 5:1).[3]

This issue presented a crisis that required attention. Paul, accompanied by Barnabas and Titus, visited Jerusalem again in order to clarify his position on the matter. About fourteen years had passed since his earlier visit with Peter and James. Paul met privately with those leaders in Jerusalem who were held in high esteem in order to make his preaching and practice clear, "lest somehow [he] should be running or had run in vain" (Gal. 2:2).[4] Although Paul wanted to gain approval for his gospel from the pillars of the Jerusalem church, he stressed that his message was not derived from them or from any man—it had come from a revelation of Jesus Christ (Gal. 1:12). Paul would not submit for a moment to those Judaizers who would make the Law mandatory for Gentile Christians, because he believed the justification of a sinner by faith would be forfeited. In spite of this conflict between Paul and the more conservative Jewish Christians, those leaders who met with Paul in executive session basically agreed with him. Specifically, Peter, John, and James gave to Paul and Barnabas the right hand of fellowhsip as a sign of their approval of his message and mission. It was then that Paul was requested to "remember the poor" (Gal. 2:10).[5]

Paul saw in the collection an opportunity to vindicate himself in the eyes of those who remembered him primarily as a persecutor of Christianity. The money that he brought for the poor would demonstrate the sincerity of his commitment to Jesus as the Christ and to that community formed by faith in him. To

those Jews who interpreted Paul's doctrine of justification by
faith apart from works of the law as antinomianism and a threat
to the stability of Jewish society, the collection could also serve
as an overt sign of Paul's continuing love for his own nation (cf.
Rom. 9:1–5). But, most important of all, Paul felt that this was
an opportunity to weld together his work in the Diaspora with
the mother church in Jerusalem. As long as Paul's gospel was
held in question, any churches he founded were suspect. If the
collection proved successful, a potential split between Jewish
and Gentile Chrisitanity could be forestalled and the unity of
Christianity expressed symbolically if not realized in fact. With
such a prospect in view Paul was eager to respond to the needs
of the poor in Jerusalem.

The Method

Paul began to announce the collection to those churches he
had founded and put into effect a program to insure that the
needed funds would be raised. While he contacted churches in
Galatia, Asia, and Macedonia, his correspondence with Corinth
in Achaia offers the clearest knowledge of his method of fund
raising. Passing through the Roman province of Galatia, on
what is often referred to as his third missionary journey, Paul
arrived at Ephesus in Asia during the summer of A.D. 52 and
stayed until the fall of 54. During this time he wrote to Corinth
the "previous letter" mentioned in 1 Corinthians 5:9 and an-
nounced the collection. The Corinthians, realizing that Paul
was staying just across the Aegean Sea, replied with a letter in
which they asked Paul several questions about how they should
conduct themselves as Christians (1 Cor. 7:1). This correspondence from Corinth was supplemented by a report from
Chloe's people (1 Cor. 1:11) and also by a visit from Stephanas,
Fortunatus, and Achaicus (1 Cor. 16:17). Their letter appears to
have asked additional information about how the collection
should be raised because, in addressing himself to this matter,

Paul used his customary phrase in responding to their questions: "Now concerning."

He instructed the Corinthians to follow the same policy that
he had directed the Galatian churches to observe (1 Cor. 16:1).
On the first day of every week, each Christian was to set aside
at home an amount of money proportionate to how he had
prospered.[6] Then, when Paul arrived, the funds would be ready
and no collection in haste or under duress would be necessary.
The church at Corinth was comprised primarily of members of
the lower class (1 Cor. 1:26–29). Given the limitations of their
financial resources, the church could not contribute a large sum
at one given time. However, by saving weekly, in a year this
regular small amount could become a relatively generous sum.

When Paul arrived at Corinth, the church would select its
representatives to take their contribution to Jerusalem. These
representatives would be certified by a letter from the brethren
to the church in Jerusalem, this epistle serving as their representatives' credentials. It would be expected to contain a Christian greeting, an expression of filial affection and concern for
the poor, an admission of prayers on behalf of the Jerusalem
church, an introduction of the representatives, and the amount
of the Corinthians' contribution.

2. The Collection at Corinth

While Paul continued his work in Ephesus, word reached him
that some members of the Corinthian church were resentful of
his authority and suspicious of the fund-raising campaign. Paul
dispatched Titus with a harsh letter in order to put down this
opposition, a letter penned with "much affliction and anguish
of heart and with many tears" (2 Cor. 2:4). Titus was successful
in temporarily reconciling the Corinthians with Paul and added
some impetus to the collection program. However, before Paul
heard of Titus' success, he left Ephesus in the fall of 54; after

some difficulty and anxiety he met with Titus in Macedonia.
Greatly encouraged by Titus' optimistic report, Paul moved to
keep the momentum of the fund drive. He wrote a letter, 2
Corinthians 1—9, exhorting the Corinthians to continue the
collection and sent the letter and Titus back to Corinth.[7] Accompanying Titus were two other advance men who were responsible for raising the much-needed money. One brother
who was a famous evangelist was expected to move the Corinthians to greater generosity. Another "proven brother,"
whose integrity would not be easily impugned, lent the quality
of unimpeachable honesty to the collection.[8] "We intend," Paul
said, "that no one should blame us about this liberal gift which
we are administering, for we aim at what is honorable not only
in the Lord's sight but also in the sight of men" (2 Cor. 8:20–21;
cf. Rom. 12:17).

The Theological Ground

Paul's appeal to the Corinthians to give reveals much of his
own theology and personality. The importance of the collection, not only as a symbol of Christian unity but also as an act
of fellowship that would actually create unity, made it impera-
tive for Paul that the amount be adequate. He therefore used
well-calculated means of persuasion in order to obtain a sub-
stantial gift. These inducements are set forth in 2 Corinthians
7—9. Paul began by half apologizing for the harsh letter that he
had previously written to Corinth (2 Cor. 7:8–13). He admitted
that he was sorry that it had been necessary to write it and
regretted the grief it had caused them. But since the letter and
Titus' skillful work as liaison had prompted them to repent and
reaffirm their loyalty to Paul, the outcome proved the wisdom
of his stern message. Therefore Paul now rejoiced.

Having made amends for the anger and disappointment
couched in his earlier epistle, Paul spelled out the theological
ground for Christian giving. He looked to the incarnation as the

focal point for divine grace and as an example of Christian love
and ethical conduct. "For you know the grace of our Lord Jesus
Christ, that though he was rich, yet for your sake he became
poor, so that by his poverty you might become rich" (2 Cor. 8:9).
By speaking of "rich" and "poor" Paul did not mean the economic conditions in which Jesus lived. In fact, Paul's letters
reveal virtually no interest in the historical Jesus beyond the
events of the Passion Week. The poverty of Christ should be
understood in keeping with the kenotic passage of Philippians
2:4–11. It is the preexistent Lord of whom Paul wrote, who,
though he was in the form of God, did not grasp at equality with
God but emptied himself and identified himself completely
with the human condition, even coming under the demonic
powers that frustrate human existence.

Not only did Christ Jesus take the form of a servant, he was
born in the likeness of men; he learned obedience through his
sufferings, which brought him to the death on the cross. It was
this self-giving love, active in the interest of others, that Paul
saw as the example to be emulated by every man who exalted
Jesus as Lord. It was the mind of Christ that he admonished
Christians to manifest, because they were "in Christ" when his
love guided their lives. The church, the body of Christ, was the
corporate expression of the new creation—a new humanity
where love controlled all interpersonal relations and acted for
the well-being of one's fellows.[9] "Let each of you look not only
to his own interests, but also to the interest of others" (Phil. 2:4).

It was to the love of God, who responded to man's need for
salvation and who acted through the incarnation and crucifixion, that Paul appealed in order to motivate the Corinthians to
give (1 Cor. 2:2). The Divine Sovereign through his grace re-
deemed mankind from the evil powers in the world that thwart
authentic human life (Rom. 8:31–39). The Christian lived as a
new man in a new age formed by the sovereign love of God that
was revealed in the Cross (Rom. 8:18–30; 2 Cor. 5:17–20). Salvation meant the acknowledgement of God's love as the forma-

tive power of the new age. Therefore, one could no longer
maintain a separation of the spiritual and the material, because
in the new age the love of God would recreate the old world
into the new. Consequently the Christian's money must be
expended in the service of love or, better, in the interest of
others. To separate the spiritual and material as though they
were two distinct spheres was to repeat the dualism of the
Gnostic heretics and those spiritualists at Corinth that opposed
Paul (2 Cor. 11:1–6; 1 Cor. 14:1–33).[10] To refuse the demands of
love as presented in the needs of another, especially a brother
in Christ, is to reject love as sovereign (Gal. 6:10). Paul was not
so naïve as to think that the man of faith would be perfectly
transformed into a loving individual. The Christian would continue to live by God's grace and must never cease trusting God
as the source of forgiveness and authentic life (Rom. 5:1–5).
Though the believer may desire to do what is good, he can not
perform accordingly (Rom. 7:13–25). But to presume upon
God's grace as an excuse for apathy toward others in need and
for the selfish pursuit of one's own business is a denial of Christ
as Lord (Rom. 6).[11]

Love naturally finds expression in concrete deeds of service,
but charity given without love is valueless. In 1 Corinthians 13:3
Paul stated that if one gave away all he had—even allowing his
body to be burned—but did not act in love, he accomplished
nothing. It was not their possessions but the Corinthians that
Paul sought to possess for Christ (2 Cor. 8:5, 12:14). When they
had surrendered themselves to Christ their money would be
used consistently with their commitment. Love prompts the
Christian to respond freely and cheerfully to the needs of others; love does not see deprivation as a deplorable condition to
be avoided. Need is the opportunity for love to respond crea-
tively.

Paul insisted that the Corinthians not contribute reluctantly
as though the collection were exacted under compulsion (2 Cor.
9:7). Each Christian could determine for himself the appropri-

ate amount to give. This decision would take into consideration
the seriousness of the exigency, the resources at hand, and
family responsibilities. No certain amount or percentage is suggested by Paul, "for if the readiness is there, it is acceptable
according to what a man has, not according to what he has not"
(2 Cor. 8:12).

A deep sense of community solidarity and mutual responsibility helped them to understand the significance of the collection.
The reciprocal care existing between brethren and churches
insured against their becoming destitute. When one church was
depressed, those Christians who could rallied to support it with
material supplies. When the economic conditions were reversed, funds would flow back in the direction of the greater
need. So it was in the family of God. The point was not that
some Christians should be burdened while others lived in ease.
Love seeks to respond effectively to lack and fill the void both
with love itself and those material manifestations of love's presence. Paul said "that as a matter of equality your abundance at
the present time should supply their want, so that their abundance may supply your want, that there may be equality" (2
Cor. 8:14). He did not mean that the goal of the Christian community was to establish an equal distribution of goods, but
rather that Christians should care equally for one another
through specific deeds of compassion.[12] This was the equality of
love in action to supply every necessity. For if the Corinthians
had come to share in the spiritual blessings emanating from
Jerusalem, they in turn should serve the mother church in
material blessings (Rom. 15:27; cf. 15:1–3).

Practical Persuasion

Notwithstanding the theological ground for the collection,
Paul encouraged the Corinthians by a few pragmatic fund-raising techniques. He established a spirit of competition between
the Macedonian and Achaian churches. He may well have

revived a sense of regional competition that could be traced back to the fourth century B.C., when Philip of Macedon united all of Greece under his rule and laid the foundation for his son, Alexander the Great, to conquer the decaying Persian Empire in a decade. However Paul did not crassly set quotas for each church. He rather presented the churches with the opportunity to demonstrate the measure of their faith through their contribution to the poor in Jerusalem.

Paul began by expressing his own high esteem for the Corinthian Christians and affirming his confidence in their dedication to Christ. He had expressed this pride earlier to Titus, before he was sent to Corinth (2 Cor. 7:14–16). The Corinthians had vindicated Paul's boasting by their warm reception of Titus and by their reaffirming their zeal for Paul. Now Paul bragged directly to the Corinthians concerning their ability to excel in every area of Christian service, "in faith, in utterance, in knowledge, in all earnestness, and in your love for us" (2 Cor. 8:7). Then he told them to excel also in giving cash.[13]

To the churches of Macedonia Paul held up the Corinthians as examples of the faithful, telling them that Achaia has been prepared for a year to make an offering. The picture he drew of Achaian liberality inspired the Macedonians to want to participate in the relief program. Paul said that the Macedonians went so far as to beg him for the opportunity to contribute to this worthy cause. But, he added, it was not simply money that they gave; they made the supreme sacrifice by first giving "themselves to the Lord and to us by the will of God" (2 Cor. 8:5; cf. Rom. 12:1–2). For they had come to see this fellowship as an expression of the worldwide Christian community. The wealth of liberality on the part of the Macedonians could not be explained by their abundant resources. Paul stated that it was rather in their extreme poverty that they had given, not just as they had prospered but even beyond their means. Paul upheld the poor's right to give what they could because he recognized that love seeks opportunity to share. This the Macedonians had done in imitation of the self-sacrificial love revealed in the Cross, and they were grateful for the opportunity to reflect that love that was the ground of their existence.

Since the Corinthians had been presented to these most liberal Macedonians as an example of Christian generosity, Paul admonished them to let their contribution be a proof both of their faith and his boasting (2 Cor. 8:24). Then Paul implicitly threatened the Corinthians concerning what would happen if they failed in the collection (2 Cor. 9:1–5). He reminded them that he would make a personal visit hard on the heels of Titus and the two other advance men. With Paul would be those Macedonian brethren selected by their respective churches to convey their offering to Jerusalem. These men had been informed by Paul of the Corinthians' munificence. He envisioned his own personal embarrassment at the encounter if, after having inspired the Macedonians with boasts of the Corinthians' liberality, the Corinthians themselves had proven niggardly. This would be a double disappointment, for not only would Paul's confidence in the Corinthians be shattered, he would appear a fool in the eyes of the Macedonians for having been so gullible. But, further, Paul warned the Corinthians of their own humiliation if those liberal and generous Macedonians should come to find the Corinthians unprepared. The Corinthians' chagrin would be especially keen, since they had been used as the example of liberality that had encouraged the Macedonians to contribute beyond their means. So Paul appealed to the Corinthians to complete the collection that they had begun the previous year and to fulfill the purpose that they had made (2 Cor. 8:10, 9:3).

Finally, Paul stated the benefits that would accrue to the Corinthians through their participation in the relief. While they would know that their service supplied a critical lack among the Jerusalem saints, further, the mother church would overflow with thanksgiving to God in the Corinthians' behalf. The mission churches, whose very existence was made possible by the

Gospel radiating from the Holy City, could now in some measure repay their spiritual blessings by sending material blessings
in return. But this cash donation would be transformed into
prayers of thanksgiving before God. Since God supplies all gifts,
both spiritual and material, there should be no anxiety over
being left without the necessities of life. Indeed, the willingness
to be munificent and joyful springs from an abiding trust in God
as the sustainer of authentic life. Paul believed that God can and
does enrich the man of faith in every way (2 Cor. 9:10–15). "And
God is able to provide you with every blessing in abundance,
so that you may always have enough of everything and may
provide in abundance for every good work. As it is written, 'He
scatters abroad, he gives to the poor; his righteousness endures
for ever' " (2 Cor. 9:8–9; Ps. 112:9; cf. Phil. 4:19; 1 Tim. 6:17–19).

3. The Value of Work

Paul's efforts to raise money at Corinth left him vulnerable to
the criticism of his opponents. Some cast aspersions on Paul's
integrity and insinuated, if not directly charged, that Paul was
planning to embezzle the funds.[14] Some maligned Paul by
charging that he was crafty and took advantage of the Corinthians by guile (2 Cor. 12:16). Paul was well aware of the impact on
the collection of these attempts to vilify him and tried to overcome such suspicions through the way he had organized the
campaign. He had asked the Corinthians to select representatives to carry their contribution to Jerusalem (1 Cor. 16:3–4).
Those men, such as Titus and the brother famous for his preaching, had been picked by Paul as men of impeccable reputation.
Another criticism raised by Paul's antagonists at Corinth was
that he was obviously not a genuine apostle and knew it, since
he refrained from taking any support for his preaching. Paul
was at pains to explain that he did not claim support for his
personal needs because he did not wish to burden them; it was

not because he did not have the right or because he did not love them (1 Cor. 9:3–18; 2 Cor. 11:7–11).

Paul further defended himself by appealing to his previous conduct at Corinth, when he had given no indication that he was greedy for money. On the contrary, Acts says that he had worked hard with his own hands in order to be self-supporting. Paul did not wish to be a financial liability to this mission congregation and had preached the Gospel to them without cost (2 Cor. 11: 7, 9, 12:13, 16). At Corinth Paul stayed with Aquila, a native of Pontus who had recently been expelled from Rome by Claudius, and his wife Priscilla, because they and Paul were tentmakers (Acts 18:1–4).[15] Paul no doubt had learned this trade while a boy from his father in Tarsus and he followed the accepted rabbinic custom of not wishing to make material gain from his teaching God's will.

Paul set an example of industry and independence. He preached a gospel of salvation by faith apart from the works of the law (Rom. 3:27–31). He believed all of man's efforts to commend himself by his own good works to be useless before God, "for no human being will be justified in [God's] sight by works of the law since through the law comes knowledge of sin" (Rom. 3:20). However, the man of faith who has experienced God's love is motivated to share this love with others. God's love is not an excuse for idleness but a reason to work. In comparing his own way of life to that of the other apostles, Paul declared that he worked harder than any of them, although it was not his work now but rather the grace of God working through him (1 Cor. 15:10; Rom. 15:17–18). One needs only to trace Paul's extensive travels as a missionary in order to get some idea of the energy he put forth to fulfill his vocation.

Paul also stressed that the Christian should be independent. Love seeks to help rather than to be a burden. "Owe no one anything, except to love one another; for he who loves his neighbor has fulfilled the law" (Rom. 13:8). Paul's correspondence with the church at Thessalonica bears out his emphasis

on the necessity for the Christian to work. He claimed that at
Thessalonica he had worked night and day, along with Silvanus
and Timothy, in order not to be a burden to the church while
they preached the Gospel (1 Thess. 2:9; 2 Thess. 3:7–9). Paul
called on the Thessalonians to imitate their example. He told
them to mind their own affairs, and to work with their hands
in order to be dependent on nobody (1 Thess. 4:11–12; 2 Thess.
3:12). Their diligence would not only gain them the respect of
the outsider, but would increase their capacity to help the weak
and "to do good to one another and to all" (1 Thess. 5:15; cf. Eph.
4:28).

Concerning those who were idle and unwilling to work Paul
gave specific instructions. They should be admonished to follow
Paul's example of industry and independence (1 Thess. 5:14). If
they persisted in their refusal to work and continued to be idle
busybodies, Paul instructed the Thessalonians to exclude them
from their fellowship, especially their table fellowship. "If any
one will not work, let him not eat" (2 Thess. 3:6, 10). Paul did
not commend the value of industry as though it were itself good
and idleness evil. He rather tried to correct a situation where
some burdened others unnecessarily by their indolence. It is
not an act of love to impose on the generosity of another. Neither did Paul advocate that the Thessalonians be self-reliant
when he admonished them to be economically independent.
For Paul, all of life was grounded in the sovereign love of God
revealed in the Cross; the Christian lives in the full awareness
that he stands only by grace and not by his own works. In this
knowledge, however, the believer seeks in his limited way to
share God's love.

The importance that Paul attached to being financially independent did not, however, prevent him from accepting assistance from those disposed to offer it. He did not possess the pride
of self-reliance that would make him reluctant to receive support from anyone. However, he told the Corinthians that he
would not accept their money for his own personal needs; this

was in order to silence those who impugned his honesty concerning the collection (2 Cor. 11:9–11). But on several occasions Paul did take money for his maintenance from the church in Philippi (2 Cor. 11:9; Phil. 4:10–20). He was grateful to them and to God for the material supplies that they continually sent. Their physical assistance pleased Paul, even though he had learned to be content in want as well as in plenty. But Paul was no ascetic, and when a windfall came his way he could be thankful to God for prosperous times. No doubt the support of the Philippians not only encouraged Paul, but also provided him with the opportunity to concentrate more fully on his missionary work free from financial problems. However, it was not just having his physical needs supplied that pleased him; he recognized that their support was an expression of their care for him and appreciation for the work he performed. Therefore he accepted their offering as an affirmation of their fellowship and common faith. Paul recognized that his need offered the opportunity for their love to act, and love in action was the essence of the Christian's life. He said, "Not that I seek the gift; but I seek the fruit which increases to your credit" (Phil. 4:17). In Acts Paul quoted Jesus' statement: " 'It is more blessed to give than to receive' "(20:35).

4. The Results of the Collection

The results of the collection in accomplishing Paul's objectives are difficult to assess. His own letters suggest some trepidation on his part as to what would happen once he reached Jerusalem. Following the writing of 2 Corinthians 1—9 from Macedonia and the return trip of Titus and his two companions to Corinth, Paul also made his promised visit to the Isthmus City. It was during the winter of 54 while he stayed in Achaia that Paul wrote his epistle to the Romans. He informed the Roman church of his proposed mission in Spain and explained

that he hoped to see them on his way to the western end of the
Mediterranean. But first he had to convey the contributions of
the Macedonians and Achaians for the poor of Jerusalem (Rom.
15:22–29).

Paul had a premonition of what would transpire in Jerusalem.
He requested the Roman Christians to pray for him on two
accounts (Rom. 15:30–31): first, that he would be delivered from
the "unbelievers" in Judea; second, that his service for the
Jerusalem saints would be acceptable.[16] After all, the collection
was primarily to demonstrate to the Jerusalem Christians the
loyalty and unity of Paul's mission churches to the mother
church. If the collection seemed small in their eyes, it would but
confirm the suspicions of his opponents.

Acts indicates that Paul's fears were well founded. Even
before he left Corinth there was a conspiracy against him (Acts
20:1–6). In Paul's company were a number of representatives of
the churches in Galatia, Asia, and Macedonia who were helping
him carry the collection to Jerusalem. When they were about
to set sail for Syria a plot against Paul by the Jews was uncov-
ered, and Paul and his associates made a strategic retreat back
to Macedonia. The motive for the plot is not given, but the
considerable sum of money in Paul's possession could well add
incentive. Embarking from Philippi, Paul sailed down the Asian
coast of the Aegean Sea and then on to Palestine (Acts 20:6 ff.).

When Paul arrived in Jerusalem the brethren received him
gladly—and no doubt the funds as well. They immediately
warned Paul of the threat to his safety. There were thousands
of Jews who had accepted Jesus as the messiah but continued
zealously to observe the Law of Moses. The report was being
circulated that Paul's gospel of salvation by faith apart from
works of the law was equivalent to antinomianism, and hence
threatened their religious traditions as well as the stability of
their society. In order to defuse this explosive situation, the
brethren encouraged Paul to take a vow with four other Jews,
pay for their expenses, purify himself, and shave his head.[17] This

action would be an overt testimony that he was not attempting to destroy Jewish custom or to impugn the Law of Moses (cf. Rom. 7:7–12, 13:8–10). Although Paul made this conciliatory gesture, it was to no avail.

When some Jews from Asia saw Paul with Trophimus, a Greek from Ephesus, they trumped up the charge that Paul had committed a sacrilege by taking Trophimus into the temple. The ensuing riot resulted in Paul's being taken and held in custody until the nature of the charge could be determined. Several preliminary hearings before both Jewish and Roman officials determined nothing, and Paul was eventually transferred under heavy escort to the Roman governor's palace at Caesarea. There he was arraigned before the governor, Felix. In making his defense, Paul mentioned that he had gone to Jerusalem not to cause trouble but to bring alms and offerings for his nation (Acts 24:17). Hearing this and questioning the nature of the charges against Paul, Felix treated him considerately and postponed making any immediate judgment in the hope that Paul would give him money in return for his freedom. But no money was forthcoming. Either the brethren in Jerusalem could not or would not bail Paul out of prison. Paul eventually appealed to Caesar, and the closing chapters of Acts tell of Paul's voyage to Rome where tradition says that he was martyred during the Neronian persecution (A.D. 64). This was a few brief years before the mother church virtually vanished from the pages of history following the devastation of Jerusalem by the armies of Titus (A.D. 70).

Paul's own personal desire to vindicate himself, his gospel, and his mission churches in the sight of the Jerusalem Christians was never realized. Yet the spirit of sharing and unity that he generated in those churches strengthened them in "the grace of the Lord Jesus Christ and the love of God and the fellowship of the Holy Spirit" (2 Cor. 13:14). For it was to be through those churches established in the Diaspora that Christianity was to survive and flourish.

V

A Theology of Poverty

1. The Affluent Society

The relevance of the life and teachings of Jesus and the faith of the early church for the contemporary problems of poverty is difficult to assess. Simple solutions betray the competence of the thinker rather than the vitality of the early Christian faith or the complexity of the present situation. Yet the morass of difficulties created by efforts to care for the poor challenges Christians to achieve a new perspective and a fresh approach in relating effectively to poor people. The New Testament offers this new though radical perspective. The angle of vision it presents does not yield a simplistic solution, but rather points in a direction that offers genuine hope to those who will journey in faith. What relevance does such a faith have for contemporary society? In order to answer this question it is first well to sketch very briefly the current situation.

America is a materialistic society.[1] It has been committed to those virtues that yield economic prosperity: free enterprise, individual initiative and industry, competition, capitalism, and economic imperialism. Americans take pride in being the wealthiest nation in the world, with an annual gross national product in excess of one trillion dollars. It is a nation of merchants and entrepreneurs consuming an excessive degree of the world's wealth. But this has not always been true.

Those over forty years old have vivid memories of the depression years of the thirties, when want and deprivation were common experiences. The nation roused itself from virtual bankruptcy only to be drawn into the Second World War. The wartime economy produced, along with military arms, rationing and domestic economizing. Following the war the United States emerged as a leading world power and launched into a period of unequaled and sustained prosperity. Those who had long dreamed of a better life free of deprivation and insecurity now found this dream within their grasp. Those who were able to moved to fulfill their dream: a home in the suburbs, furnishings, a car or two or three, protection from financial reversal, and an education for their children. These were things that they had been denied earlier. They moved up in income and out to suburbia. Their success was due to a combination of qualities: intelligence, initiative, health, and race. The mark of a successful man became the economic status that he achieved; so material trappings became status symbols that determined a man's importance. For example, how do most Americans answer the question, what is he worth?

Generalizations concerning the American church scene are difficult. But a trend has emerged in American church life that is obvious to even the casual observer. The churches have followed this shift to the suburbs and have abandoned the inner city.[2] This transition was not so much intentional as convenient. In the new neighborhoods new church buildings were erected, the construction and quality of which were commensurate with the homes in the community. After all, they thought, should not the church building be at least equal in quality and comfort to the houses in which we live? To build less expensive church edifices would indicate a lack of genuine Christian concern for the work and life of the church. The two decades following the Second World War saw an unequaled boom in church construction. Billions of dollars were expended on beautiful buildings—

sanctuaries, educational facilities, fellowship halls, kitchens, and recreational facilities. In some cases the splendor of the church plant became a symbol in the community of the prestige of the church and its annual budget a mark of its success. Church leaders were drawn from the successful men of the community whose sense of values was not in radical conflict with the culture's materialistic understanding of success. Ministers were sought who could help to build up the church in numbers, attendance, and size of the budget. Naturally everyone knew that these were not the true marks of the church, but when other measures of Christian growth were in question, these criteria were accepted as indicators of progress.

The poor were isolated largely because of the economic pattern of housing. But it would be disconcerting to concentrate on the poor in the midst of worship services, religious functions, and church suppers. If anyone noticed the great disparity between professing loyalty to Jesus of Nazareth and living in comfort and luxury in proximity to people who were hungry and poor, they did not speak out—for a long time.

2. The Culture of Poverty

Left increasingly farther behind were those unable to function effectively in the new period of economic growth. Factors that contributed to the exclusion of many from prosperity were obsolete skills, lack of education, age, race, and ill health. The poor suffer from a cycle of forces that generate and sustain the conditions of poverty. Ill health results from improper diet and inadequate medical care, which has been reserved primarily for those able to pay. Many children suffer brain damage as a result of malnutrition during the first year of infancy. They live in a situation that is not culturally stimulating and respond slowly to learning situations. The deprived acquire a poor self-image and little motivation, since in a society of material values being poor is equated with being worthless. The welfare check may well reinforce these feelings of inadequacy, even though it is intended to relieve human suffering. Frequently the poor resent the social conditions that have deprived them of the opportunity to participate in the affluent society. They consider a society unjust that has excluded them from a fair share. Some are driven to use violence in order to obtain those things that they have been forced to do without. They consider working in an unjust society foolish when it exploits them by low wages, with the profits going to those already secure. For these people, welfare, robbing, and even begging are better than working, since one can obtain something from the unjust society without contributing anything to it.

The churches of the poor tended to follow two quite separate courses. On the one hand biblical images were taken quite literally and heaven held up as that future reward for the "good people." There all injustices and sufferings would be banished in "that city that lies foursquare." Religion as such became an opiate to relieve present suffering and disappointment with the bright hope for a full life in the next world. On the other hand the Gospel was used as a tool by some ministers seeking social change and even revolution to accomplish their goal of a more equal distribution of wealth. Many churches became centers for organizing the poor in an effort to coerce social change and to share in the wealth of the nation.[3] In the hands of these ministers the social goal of gaining a greater share of wealth was already determined and the Gospel used as a means to attain this end.

3. The Apocalyptic Matrix

It is to this cultural situation that the faith of the early church must be addressed. However difficult the present problem, the message of the first Christians contains a radical view that may

bring a new and helpful perspective. They had experienced the
exclusion and rejection of the controlling class of their day.
They spoke for the poor and disfranchised, though they did not
limit their message to a single class. But one basic question
cannot be avoided: Can a word spoken in the relatively simple
culture of the first century be heard above the din of modern
technology and the second industrial revolution?[4] Further, if
the word could be heard and even understood, what use would
its meaning serve for the gigantic social problems of the seven-
ties?

The chasm between the early church and the present appears to yawn even wider with the full realization that faith was
informed by the apocalyptic belief that the world was in the
control of demonic powers that thwarted man's efforts to obtain
genuine life. The apocalyptists despaired of the present evil age
and longed for some divine cataclysmic intervention to destroy
forcibly the demonic powers and usher in the awaited new age.
Their symbolic language and strange images sound remote to
modern ears until one penetrates their symbols to understand
and experience the existential stance that their language reveals.[5] Then modern man discovers himself surprisingly attune
to these voices from the past. For he, too, experiences the frus-
tration, if not the futility, of his works, the loss of meaning, the
indelibility of evil, and the loneliness and alienation of life.
Demonic powers are indeed felt in the varied social problems:
the exploitation of the weak, the economic crises at home and
abroad, domestic unrest over international relations, and the
protests against the military-industrial complex.

It was against the apocalyptists' grim and pessimistic ap-
praisal of the world that Jesus and the early church proclaimed
a message of hope. Jesus was poor. His ministry was directed
primarily toward the outcasts of society and his followers drawn
largely from the lower class. His message was rooted in the
apocalyptic conviction that God was breaking into history and
was drawing near to men as Father. The standards by which

men judged one another must give way to the reign of God, where acceptance and love were the basis for a new community. The ministry of Jesus was itself a sign that the new day was dawning. Demonic powers that thwarted authentic life were placed on the defensive with the coming of the Kingdom of God. The presence of God's reign was surprising. Jesus' disciples discovered that it was in their midst as they defined their fellowship in terms of his way of life. And they were convinced that this unimpressive beginning would have an astonishing result.

The reign of God that Jesus proclaimed demanded radical reforms, both social and religious. People were more important than possessions, and human needs took precedence over religious forms. It was against the established religious leaders that Jesus directed his sharpest invectives because these hypocrites did not bridge the gap between teaching and doing. Indeed, religious traditions and observances were often more oppressive than liberating to the common man. The cleansing of the temple was a vivid announcement that the reign of God demanded reforms that overturned existing values and shook the foundations of the present social order. The fellowship that Jesus extended was the basis of the new community where genuine love for one another permeated every interpersonal relation. So Jesus healed the sick, fed the hungry, forgave sinners, and proclaimed good news to the poor. His conduct provided the context in which his message must be interpreted. Those who believed him, and in him, rejoiced at the prospect of life in the kingdom. Those whose authority was threatened by his teaching and following put him to a criminal's death on the Cross in the name of Jewish law and Roman order.

The early church was inspired by Jesus' vision of a new age and nurtured his spirit of fellowship in a community where life and goods were shared. The first Christians did not deny the reality of evil, because the Cross itself manifested the strength of demonic forces. But the Cross also disclosed a power of a different order than that which appeared to control the world. In the ministry and death of Jesus was revealed a compassion and concern for men that disclosed a love divine. His life revealed that power that is the ground of being, the source of all authentic human existence or, as John expressed it, the logos. The quality of his love was manifest in acts of concern: ministering to human needs, accepting the unacceptable, and forgiving the sinful. His miracles were viewed not as the raw display of power but in terms of the purpose that power served. The church rejoiced in the conviction that the love that Jesus disclosed was sovereign over all mankind and that they shared in its initial victory. The Christians comprised that community that exalted Jesus as Lord and dedicated itself not only to accepting love for themselves but sharing this love with one another and potentially with every man. The church was the body of Christ as the spirit of his life gave vitality to their existence. The early Christians lived at the dawn of a new age in which they believed the meaning and purpose of life had already been revealed. Those then who acknowledged Jesus as Lord were the nucleus of the new age and a witness to the world of its final destiny.

The church moved from this theological conviction to put into practice its implications. The acceptance of the kerygma required the implementation of a new economic order and social experiment, as has been fully described. The apostle Paul extended the basic insight that Christian fellowship could not be separated from the sharing of material things. He saw in the collection for the poor in Jerusalem a concrete witness to the oneness of the universal church.

4. Challenge for the Church

There is always a tension between Christ and culture[6] as the church seeks to find its place *in* the world without being *of* the world. There is a serious danger that the church of an affluent society will simply mirror its cultural values and forfeit its birthright. When the church follows the dictates of society it becomes impotent to influence changes for the better. The vital voice of the church speaking out for a more humane and just society becomes only an echo of what the culture is saying. The church is in particular jeopardy when it appears by worldly standards to be flourishing. The warning of the Christian Apocalypse is apropos for a wealthy church without genuine compassion: "For you say, I am rich, I have prospered, and I need nothing; not knowing that you are wretched, pitiable, poor, blind, and naked" (Rev. 3:17). These words were addressed to Laodicea not because the church was heretical or in league with the anti-Christ but because the Christians were lukewarm. They took pride in their prosperity rather than in the quality of their mercy.

There is, however, the very real danger that the church faced by staggering social need could forsake the proclamation of the word in order to "serve tables." It would be tragic if the church lost its identity and became only another social action group or welfare organization. The solution to this danger is not found by redoubling evangelical fervor and preaching the Gospel in a louder voice. The word of God in acts of service is an equally articulate expression of the Gospel message. It is the cup of cold water given in his name that testifies to the essence of the Christian faith. The church must make the word active in love. The teaching and ministry of Jesus are ample testimony of this way.

Granting the great demand of the Gospel, there is almost instinctively the desire to limit the sphere of those whom love should serve. Like modern lawyers we stand to ask, "Who is my neighbor?" And again the answer comes that the true disciple is called to take his stance in the world as a neighbor and brother to his fellow man. Being neighborly means reaching across social barriers such as class, race, and even religion to

minister to the individual in need. For every man is a neighbor
to the one who is himself called to be neighborly.

But if a man is lazy and prodigal, obviously unworthy of help,
should he also be given charity? Won't material assistance contribute to his indolence and increase his dependence? Won't
the Christians' good intentions be exploited by the indolent
man who takes pride in getting something for nothing? The
Christian might better bear the financial loss of his charity than
the knowledge that he has played into the hands of a profes-
sional welfare seeker. There is risk in loving another, and the
Christian need not make naïveté a virtue. The dove's harmless-
ness need not be opposed to the serpent's wisdom. The Gospel
is fundamentally a message of grace by which one is granted an
acceptance that he does not merit. The church is a community
that acknowledges unmerited love as the source of its existence
and is called to express this meaning to all men. Love is not
limited by the worth of the recipient just as it is not grounded
in the man who shares it. Love is grounded in God, for God is
love. The so-called unworthy man is an opportunity for love to
act. The one loving is not himself worthy, but he abides in God
when he loves his fellow.

The purpose of the church's benevolence, beyond the immediate value of relieving human need, should be to demonstrate to the recipient and to others that living in the power of
love is a live option. And it is a summons to have a full place in
that community that makes love its aim.[7] Assistance is freely
granted and not calculated to produce conformity to certain
cultural behavior through strings attached. The goal of benevolence is not to make everyone middle class, as though middle-
class America were the measure of the good life or a substitute
for eternal life. The equality that genuine love creates is not an
equality of goods but of acceptance, forgiveness, respect, and
trust.

Charity is not predicated on the obligation that the receiver
will get a job and go to work, as though work and industry were

good in themselves. Christian work results from the concern to be useful to others. One must provide for his own; to be able to supply the needs of children and family and not respond is a denial of love. But even more, one who knows the nature of compassion realizes that it can not be contained simply within the family circle.

Love is free. The donor gives freely without stipulations. The recipient receives in freedom without obligations, except to love. He remains free to determine in his own situation how love should respond. To accept voluntary poverty as a way of life may well be the appropriate response to the needs and suffering of others. But voluntary poverty is not itself the measure of a man. One may hear the hard demand of Jesus, "Go and sell all that you have and give to the poor," and accordingly bestow all his goods to feed the poor. But if he has not love he has not learned the true meaning of discipleship. It is the use of material possessions for the welfare of others that is the basis of the Christian economy.

The institutional church today is under attack from many quarters and some prophesy its demise with a genuine sense of satisfaction. Much of the criticism is justified. There is an irreconcilable contradiction for the church to profess Jesus as Lord and not to be committed to the way of life he portrayed. One can not observe the trends of the contemporary church without a sense of alarm. The "suburban captivity" of the church has produced such accommodation to cultural values that the voice of the church judging the world and calling for reform is scarcely more than a whisper.

Interest has been focused on handsome structures in which members can meet in comfort with aesthetic surroundings while the poor, even Christian brothers, remain isolated and trapped in poverty. The church, like Dives, enjoys the blessings of an affluent society and at best gives crumbs to suffering humanity at the door. It has grown comfortable in a materialistic society and has been unwilling to acknowledge the disparity between the message of the Cross and its application. Like priest and Levite, the church has grasped at respectability in place of responsibility and has passed by on the other side of human suffering. The church has been more intent on recreation, which has distracted its members from participation in the world rather than involving its members in the ministry of reconciliation, where men isolated from one another may find rapport through a common faith and fellowship grounded in the Christ event.

There is a basic hypocrisy in claiming the Cross as the disclosure of divine love while rejecting the spirit of self-giving and sacrifice that the Cross revealed. The church has too often displayed a cross on its steeple or fashioned it in gold for admiration, but it has been reluctant to take its demand for self-sacrifice into the world. The adoration of the sign must not substitute for dedication to the love toward which Christian lives must be directed. It is not sacrifice itself that is exalted but the love for others that solicits one to lay down his life for his friends. The indifference of the church toward the poor is all the more difficult to excuse when one recognizes that much of the wealth of middle-class Christians is derived from an economic system that suppresses and exploits the poor. The structured life of the affluent is based on a competitive and materialistic society that places profits before people and suppresses the weak.

The challenge for the church today is well expressed in the following: "By this we know love, that he laid down his life for us; and we ought to lay down our lives for the brethren. But if any one has the world's goods and sees his brother in need, yet closes his heart against him, how does God's love abide in him? Little children, let us not love in word or speech but in deed and in truth" (1 John 3:16–18).

The Cross as the disclosure of love summons men to participate in the power of love through emulating the same spirit of sacrifice on behalf of others. It is a call to action. Talking or

preaching (even analyzing theological language) does not substitute for the most articulate expression of the Gospel through
deeds of service. However, the solution to the malady of the
contemporary church is not to add a poverty program as an
adjunct to an already well organized but apathetic church program. Nor is increasing the budget for benevolence the answer.
The problem goes much deeper than that. The church must
begin by examining its own life to see where it has compro-
mised its true heritage. The source of its life is through rededi-
cation to the Cross, both as an expression of infinite love and as
a demand to surrender to the power of this love. From this
stance action springs. The surrender of one's privileged place
in a materialistic and unjust society in order to share fellowship
with the oppressed may best proclaim the significance of the
incarnation. For "though he was rich, yet for your sake he
became poor, so that by his poverty you might become rich" (2
Cor. 8:9).

The demands of the Gospel for contemporary life are hard
indeed. Who can hear them? The church has generally turned
a deaf ear to cries arising from the oppressed, cries for help and
justice. The same deafness makes it impossible to listen to the
word of God. Since the radical demand for love is predicated
on the divine love revealed in the Cross, the church stands by
grace and not by works. In the awareness of its failure, the
church reaffirms its faith in forgiveness and acceptance of the
unworthy as the ground of its existence.

The Lord's Supper celebrates the experience of grace and
triumph of love over sin and evil. Only those who recognize the
reality of evil and the tragedy of man's inhumanity to man can
fully partake of his present grace and victory. Church suppers
tend to degenerate into social gatherings that have lost their
sense of evil and tragedy, and correspondingly the experience
of triumph and freedom.[8] That church that simply reflects the
values of society cannot share in the spirit of festivity that the
first Christians knew who partook of their food with glad and

generous hearts. Their agape feasts were both declarations of
their new life in Christ and practical means to feed their poor.
The daily celebration of life was appropriately expressed in
festivity. The Eucharist and the agape feast were two expressions of the same reality and were appropriately held in conjunction with one another. Would not such a celebration be
appropriate today?

It is this spirit that challenges the church today. The task of
the church is to incarnate the reality of love and compassion in
the hearts of men so that possessions will be freely used for the
common good. "For he who does not love his brother whom he
has seen, cannot love God whom he has not seen" (1 John 4:20).

Appendix: The Poor in Israel

1. The Settlement in Canaan

Prior to the Israelites' settlement in the land of Canaan they were nomadic wanderers in the semiarid regions bordering on the Dead Sea. During this period they developed no clear-cut social distinctions. The tribes moved with their flocks and herds and pitched their tents where water and pasture dictated. Each member's dignity and identity were based on blood kinship with his tribal brethren. His status stemmed from his ability to serve his kinsmen in their ongoing struggle against natural hardships and military foes. Members of the family generally shared in equal rights within a patriarchical social organization. There were no sharp divisions between rich and poor; even slaves were members of the family, and their lives were not radically different from the others in the family. Wealth was measured primarily in terms of the size of family and flocks instead of land.[1]

Social Transitions

When the Israelite tribes migrated eastward across the Jordan River and infiltrated the land of Canaan, a profound social transformation took place. The social unit was no longer the mobile tribe; their simple nomadic existence gave way to set-

tled life in villages and towns.[2] The land was parceled out
among the tribes and each family was apportioned a permanent
land grant, a heritage in the promised land. Many of the original
inhabitants were conquered and assimilated into Israel's tribal
boundaries; others continued to coexist with the new arrivals.
In the agrarian economy of Canaan, land became the primary
measure of wealth. The Israelite land reforms, which attempted
to establish an equitable distribution of real estate, resulted
initially in a somewhat similar standard of living. Each family
took care to hold and maintain its heritage and there was little
speculation in real estate. However, association with the resident Canaanites, who had developed social stratifications, influenced Israel's pattern of sedentary life. Gradually, the less
fortunate among the Israelites coalesced with the conquered
and dispossessed, and a number of poor sank to the bottom of
the social order.

The Covenant Code

In order to protect the poor from oppression and exploitation
a number of humanitarian laws were promulgated. These laws
have been preserved in a section of the Covenant Code[3] that
is contained in Exodus 20:22–23:33. The moral foundation for
these laws was based on the conviction that Yahweh was King
of the people and Lord of the land and it was Yahweh's will that
there be no abject poverty in his land. Therefore, his law qualified and limited the exploitation both of the land and the poor.
As protector of the weak and poor Yahweh prohibited the oppression of a resident foreigner or the afflicting of any widow
or orphan (Exod. 22:21–24, 23:9). Money was to be lent to a poor
fellow Israelite without interest. If his outer garment were surrendered as collateral, it must be returned before sundown lest
he be at the mercy of the night's cold (Exod. 22:25–27). Justice
was demanded in the courts of law and a man's case could not
be determined by his financial status. Bribes to blind the judge
in balancing the scales of justice were explicitly forbidden

(Exod. 23:6–8). Every seventh year the fields were to lie fallow and the olive trees and vineyards were to be unpruned and unharvested. The poor could freely eat of all that grew in this sabbatical year (Exod. 23:10–11). If a poor man could not pay his debts and was sold with his wife into slavery, they were to be released after six years of servitude (Exod. 21:1–6). This humanitarian concern for the poor was grounded not only on Yahweh's demand for justice but also upon his desire for mercy within the covenant community, a community that he had brought out of Egypt and over which he ruled as King.

2. The Monarchical Period

Following the institution of the monarchy at the end of the second millennium, the next two centuries witnessed a social revolution that widened the gap between rich and poor. King Saul's (ca. 1020–1000) modest entourage was rapidly expanded by David (ca. 1000–961), until the magnificent court of Solomon (ca. 961–922) radiated the splendor of an oriental monarch. Solomon's heavy taxation prompted the civil war that resulted in the division of the land into the northern and southern kingdoms of Israel and Judah, each with its own capital at Samaria and Jerusalem respectively. Around the king were gathered many officials, both civil and cultic, who prospered by the king's good pleasure. In addition to the luxury enjoyed at court there arose a class of avaricious businessmen who, through personal ambition, astute judgment, and frequently unscrupulous business practices, amassed large holdings of land and possessions. However, their affluence was derived at the expense of their fellow citizens, who lived in squalor.

Prophetic Social Criticism

Against the oppression of the weak and poor the prophets protested in the name of Yahweh, who required social justice. One of the most outspoken social critics was Amos, who pro-

phesied during the last years of the reign of Jeroboam II (786–
746), a time of exceptional prosperity for the northern kingdom. Though Amos espoused the cause of the poor he did not
identify himself with them; he was a herdsman from the town
of Tekoa and a part-time dresser of sycamore trees (Amos 7:14).
Coming from this rustic background, Amos set about to criticize
urban injustices. He castigated the wealthy who relaxed in the
lap of luxury and were insensitive to human suffering all about
them. The well-to-do constructed houses of hewn stone and
planted vineyards (3:15, 5:11; cf. Hos. 8:14).[4] Their houses were
furnished with ivory beds and couches. The rich enjoyed gas-
tronomical delights such as succulent lambs from the flock and
tender baby beef from the stall. They warmed their spirits with
drafts of wine from silver bowls and passed their leisure with
idle songs sung to the sound of the harp (Amos 6:4–6). Their
women anointed themselves with the finest oils, and they con-
jured up in Amos' mind the image of the sleek and contented
cows of Bashan (4:1). The powerful and prosperous had their
ease in the capital of Samaria but were not grieved over the ruin
of Joseph (Israel) (6:6).

Amos was no ascetic. His criticisms of the rich did not rest on
a belief in the evil of luxury but rather on the violation of the
covenant community. The acquisition of wealth had been
achieved by trampling "the head of the poor into the dust of the
earth" (2:7, 4:1, 5:11, 8:4). Amos complained that men were sold
into slavery for failing to pay for a pair of shoes (2:6, 8:6) or
reduced to virtual nakedness by requiring their garments as
pledges against loans (2:8). Merchants enlarged their profits by
false balances and inferior produce (8:5); their greed was like a
canker eroding their moral sensibility and social stability. The
poor could not appeal to the courts against this economic oppression because the moneyed class controlled the decisions
through the weight of their influence or bribes (2:4, 5:7, 12, 6:12).
Amos saw a kind of violence expressed through the injustices of
his society (3:10, 6:3), a violence that would not be long con-

tained but that would break forth and consume the nation. This coming destruction he proclaimed was the day of the Lord: "It is darkness and not light; as if a man fled from a lion, and a bear met him" (5:18–19). So Amos warned and entreated those who were in a position to take positive action to establish justice in the gate (5:15); "But let justice roll down like waters, and righteousness like an everflowing stream" (5:24).

Within thirty years Samaria fell (722–721) before the Assyrian army led by Sargon II, and the northern kingdom was never restored.

Meanwhile, in the southern kingdom of Judah, similar economic conditions developed paralleling those in Samaria. The royal court in Jerusalem sustained numerous officials—military, civil, and religious—who combined with the wealthy landowners and merchants to form an affluent aristocracy.[5] The urbanite Isaiah (742–700) prophesied in Jerusalem during the period of Samaria's fall and detected the same oppression that had weakened the northern kingdom. To the elders and princes he directed his interrogation in the name of Yahweh: "What do you mean by crushing my people, by grinding the face of the poor?" (Isa. 3:15). Micah (722–701), the younger contemporary of Isaiah from the small town of Moresheth-Gath, was especially sensitive to the social injustices of those who had established themselves in Jerusalem. In opposition to their military build-up Micah hoped for a disarmament when men would "beat their swords into plowshares" (Mic. 4:3). He opposed the wealthy and greedy landowners who were forcing the small farmer from his ancestral land; "they covet fields and seize them; and houses, and take them away" (Mic. 2:2; cf. 1 Kings 21). Rather, Micah envisioned a time when domestic tranquility and equitable distribution of land would be achieved and "they shall sit every man under his vine and under his fig tree, and none shall make them afraid" (Mic. 4:4). However, the vision of this utopia did not blind him to the grim realities of urban exploitation, where the weak were devoured by the strong and the poor skinned by the rich (3:2–3). He was witness to a society where covenant loyalty and social justice had been broken down by material values (6:10–12). "Money talked" through corrupt judges, priests, and prophets (3:11), and there were none before whom the weak could plead their case. Micah called for radical reforms in his summary of Hebrew prophecy: "He has showed you, O man, what is good; and what does the Lord require of you but to do justice, and to love kindness, and to walk humbly with your God?" (6:8).

The Deuteronomic Code

In the century following Isaiah and Micah the Deuteronomic Reformation did attempt to deal constructively with social abuses, though with modest success. The reformation was possible in large measure due to the decline of the Assyrian Empire, which had long dominated the kingdom of Judah.[6] King Josiah (640–609), riding a wave of nationalism, instituted a movement during the twelfth year of his reign (627) to remove all expressions of Assyrian domination and to revitalize Mosaic Yahwism (2 Chron. 34:3–7). Pagan altars were demolished and their cultic personnel removed. During the renovation of the Temple (621) a scroll was found that lent religious sanction and direction to Josiah's reform. The contents of the scroll can be inferred from the nature of the reforms based upon it and must have corresponded to Deuteronomy 12–26, the Deuteronomic Code. Not only were pagan sanctuaries destroyed and their priests defrocked, but even altars and shrines dedicated to Yahweh were proscribed and all official worship centered at the Jerusalem Temple. This resulted in the unemployment of many Levites who had officiated in local shrines outside of Jerusalem (2 Kings 23:4–20; 2 Chron. 34: 32–33). These unemployed, along with the poor and other dispossessed—sojourners, widows, and orphans —were the special concern of the humanitarian laws of the Deuteronomic Code.

The code itself contains many ancient laws and customs that were recast for the seventh century.[7] The motivation for these laws was grounded in the nature of Yahweh, who showed his mercy by delivering Israel from Egyptian bondage. Israel was, therefore, obligated to reflect Yahweh's mercy within the social order (Deut. 15:15, 24:22, 26:5–10). The Deuteronomic Code called for judicial reforms that would provide impartial decisions at the municipal courts. Each town was to establish men of integrity to render fair judgments unswayed by financial influences. "Justice, and only justice, you shall follow, that you may live and inherit the land" (16:20, 24:17). Consumer protection was sought through a system of standardized weights and measures (25:13–16). The wages of a day laborer were to be paid at the end of each work day so as not to cause him and his family any unnecessary deprivation (24:14–15).

Lending practices were regulated in order to protect the poor man's person and dignity. It was assumed that a man seeking a loan was in need; therefore, a request for a loan by a fellow Israelite should be honored and, further, should be granted without collecting the interest that could be exacted from a foreigner (23:19–20; cf. Neh. 5:1–13). The garment of a poor man taken as a pledge had to be returned at sundown so that he might have something in which to sleep (Deut. 24:12–13); a widow's garment could not be used as a pledge (24:17); neither could a millstone be taken as collateral since it would remove from the miller the means of his living. The invasion of privacy was also forbidden, as the creditor was required to stand outside the door while the debtor brought out his pledge from his own house (24:10–11). In order to prevent abject poverty in Israel that could be passed on from father to son, the Deuteronomic Code stipulated that every seventh year all debts were to be canceled and warned against niggardliness as the seventh year drew near (15:1–11). Hebrew slaves were to be released after six years of servitude and were to be provided with a liberal "grub stake" from their master's flock, grain, and wine (15:12–15).

The Deuteronomic Code also laid down laws to provide for the welfare of the poor and dispossessed. The levirate law protected a widow whose husband had died without giving her sons to care for her and the family estate. Her husband's brother (*levir* is Latin for "brother") was to take her and raise up sons in the name of her deceased husband so that the family name and inheritance "may not be blotted out of Israel" (25:6). If for any reason the living brother refused his responsibility, the elders of the city summoned him to the gate. The widow removed his sandal and spit in his face as a sign that he had shirked his duty (25:7–10; cf. Ruth 4:7–9).

Systematic distributions of food were made to the dispossessed, i.e., Levites, resident foreigners, widows, and orphans. Every third year the tithe of the produce was stored up in each city for the poor (Deut. 14:28–29, 26:12–15). Each year that the grain, olives, and grapes were harvested a portion of the yield was to be left for the poor to glean (24:19–22). Before the harvest a man was permitted to walk through his neighbor's vineyard and eat his fill of grapes but he could not gather any in a vessel. Likewise a man could eat ripening grain from his neighbor's field provided he did not use a sickle (23:24–25). The religious festivals in Judah also gave the poor opportunities each year for feasting and religious holidays (16:9–15).

The laws for the protection of the poor in the Deuteronomic Code were obviously not uniformly enforced, and their very presence suggests practices to the contrary. However, this legislation reveals social conditions in Judah in the century prior to the fall of Jerusalem to the Babylonians (587) and demonstrates that much of the prophetic social criticism was consistent with ancient covenant laws. While it was recognized that "the poor will never cease out of the land" (Deut. 15:11; cf. 15:4; Mark 14:7), the humanitarian perspective of the Deuteronomic Code sought to prevent the exploitation of the economically deprived.[8]

The Holiness Code

At about the time of the fall of Jerusalem, the Holiness Code (Lev. 17–26) was compiled. While containing a number of older humanitarian laws for the protection of the poor (i.e., 23:22, 25:3–7, 35–55), it reflects a distinctly priestly point of view. Its stress on the ethical is best summarized in the command: "You shall not take vengeance or bear any grudge against the sons of your own people, but you shall love your neighbor as yourself: I am the Lord" (19:18). An interesting feature of the Holiness Code is the proposal that a year of jubilee be celebrated every fifty years in which all land would be restored to its original family. This would prevent the permanent building up of large estates with the corresponding result of driving the small farmer from his inheritance. This idea was never seriously enacted, however.

3. The Exile

When the Babylonians captured Jerusalem (587), they carried away many of the aristocracy and artisans and devastated the land of Judah. The ensuing depression reduced the gap between rich and poor, as all suffered economic hardships. Those who retained some vestige of wealth and power continued to use it to self-advantage (Ezek. 34) and the poor were forced to the very fringe of existence. It was Deutero-Isaiah, a half-century after the fall of Jerusalem, who recognized the plight of the poor and called for acts of charity to relieve their suffering as an expression of true religion before Yahweh: "Is it not to share your bread with the hungry, and bring the homeless poor into your house; when you see the naked, to cover him, and not to hide yourself from your own flesh? Then shall your light break forth like the dawn (Isa. 58:7–8; cf. Zech. 7:8–10; Esther 9:22).

The Hebrew words for "poor" and "rich" have no moral or

religious meaning in themselves, but they acquire moral connotations along two contrasting lines of thought, which can be
illustrated from the Psalms and Proverbs. One line of thought
is consistent with the prophetic social critique. Beginning with
the experience that the poor were often oppressed by the
wicked rich, the poor were considered to be the special objects
of Yahweh's protection and deliverance (Pss. 9:18, 10:1–8, 12:5,
13:6, 34:6, 35:10, 37:14–15, 40:17, 41:1–3, 68:10, 70:5, 72:1–14, 74:-
19–21, 82:4, 86:1–2, 107:41, 109:16–31, 113:7, 132:15, 140:12; Prov.
22:22–23). Therefore the poor looked to Yahweh as the source
of deliverance from their enemies and oppressors. This attitude
of trust and dependence exemplified that piety that should
have characterized every Israelite. In this way the concept of
the "pious poor" developed.[9] A closely related idea, though less
familiar, was that deeds of charity rendered to the poor were
reflections of Yahweh's nature (Ps. 112:6–9; Prov. 14:21, 31, 19:17,
31:20; Isa. 58:6–9).

An opposing line of thought toward the poor was influenced
by the doctrine of retribution, which considered a man's economic status as an index to his virtue and God's approval (Pss.
1:1–6, 112; Prov. 15:6). Poverty was seen as the result caused by
a man's own actions whether they were wasteful (Prov. 21:20),
lazy (Prov. 6:6–11, 10:4–5), pleasure-seeking (21:17), or drunken
(21:17, 23:21). The Book of Job is an eloquent protest against the
then prevalent attitude that poverty was divine punishment for
moral failures. The righteous Job lost his riches, children, and
health, but uncompromisingly affirmed his innocence (Job 24,
29–31). The writer of Job maintained that one's physical and
economic condition was no measure of divine approval.[10]

4. Between The Testaments

Following Alexander the Great's conquest of Palestine in 332
B.C., the Jewish state experienced an extensive period of social

and political instability. After Alexander's death the Jews fell under the control of the Seleucids, whose capital was located in Syria. The Jews smoldered under the aggressive program of Hellenization carried out by Antiochus IV (Epiphanes). Finally, the fires of rebellion broke out under the leadership of the Maccabeus family. Skillful use of guerrilla tactics coupled with exceptional determination resulted in winning a peace treaty from the Syrians (165 B.C.) that provided an uneasy independence for the Jews. Their freedom lasted until Pompey arrived in 63 B.C. and brought Judea under Roman domination. This period of conflict and political unrest, both internal and external, created unfortunate economic conditions that forced many Jews into deprivation and despair. From these hardships was produced an ethos of poverty.

The reactions to poverty were not uniform. Extremists gathered members from the lowest classes and plundered the goods of others. Sectarian groups were formed identifying themselves with those poor who were precious in the sight of Yahweh, accepting their poverty as a special mark of their pious lives. A case in point is the Essenes of Qumran, who referred to themselves as "The Poor." They formed a semimonastic community and retreated to the northwest shores of the Dead Sea in order to experiment with communal living. Membership in the sect was carefully regulated and a man had to surrender all his goods to the community before being admitted.[11]

In the Apocrypha and Pseudepigrapha an eschatological understanding of the poor is preserved that interpreted their existence into the theology of history. The belief was expressed that in the age to come the poor would become rich. However, the arrival of the new age would be preceded by the struggle between good and evil forces. This conflict would encompass a class struggle in which the poor would rise up and overthrow the rich who suppressed them. This theology of poverty looked to God for deliverance rather than to social revolution.[12] Poverty could be passively accepted in the confidence that divine deliverance would come.

The conviction that the poor were special objects of divine concern reinforced the requirement for loving-kindness and almsgiving (Tob. 4:7, 16). If the Endtime were indeed drawing near, the circumspect should help lift up the poor. Charity and generosity were marks of the righteous man.[13] For example, in the "Testament of Job," it is Job's care for the poor that is stressed as a mark of the good man (Job 29:12, 16, 31:16–22, 29–32).[14]

5. Rabbinic Teachings

The jurists of the Tannaitic period continued to repeat the teachings of the Old Testament regarding the poor and interpreted these laws in a spirit of generosity that went even beyond the Old Testament's requirement. The first of the six major divisions of the Mishnah, *Zeraim* (seeds), is given over to laws for the benefit of the poor and others without means of support. During this period charity was encouraged; concern and care for the weak and deprived in the community were but reflections of the loving-kindness that God had shown his people and required of them. Indeed, to refuse to be merciful to a fellow Jew in need was judged to be the same as idolatry, since it was a denial of God's rule over the community. Therefore, both public and private charity was expected and policies were instituted to care for the poor.

The rabbis believed that charity began at home and a man's first responsibility was to members of his own immediate family and kinsfolk before his fellow citizens or strangers. The oldest juristic commentary on Deuteronomy 15:7–11 sets forth in brief the consensus of rabbinic teaching.[15] The request of a man in need should not be refused; his needs must be defined in terms of his station in life. For example, a man from a well-to-do family who had suffered financial reversal might legitimately expect more than a man of lower rank. In order to protect the pride of the recipient charity should be carried out in private. There was a room in Jerusalem adjacent to the temple, called the "chamber of the silent," where wealthy philanthropists placed relief funds and the poor of good families came and took money.[16] When charity was extended the donor was encouraged to give it as though it were a loan (that he would not attempt to collect). It was understood that the amount one should feel responsible to give was dependent on one's resources. So the principle was laid down that charity should be from each according to his ability, to each according to his need.

If alms were sought of one unable to give, he should at least express his sympathy for the poor man's plight (cf. Acts 3:6; James 2:14–17). Since eleemosynary deeds were reflections of the divine mercy, gifts to the poor were considered to make God the debtor. One should not refrain from generosity through the fear of becoming poor, because God could make proper returns. After all, the rabbis thought, a man's wealth or poverty was God's doing and he could reverse the wheel of fortune. In time of special need, such as after the war with Hadrian, especially pious Jews gave their entire estates for relief of the war victims. But the judgment was rendered that such well-meaning prodigality only increased the problem by reducing self-supporting families to abject poverty. It was consequently agreed that one should give only a fifth of his property and a fifth of his income in any given year for charity.

Public measures were also undertaken to provide for the temporarily and permanently poor. The meager evidence from the first century A.D. yields to rather clearly defined municipal relief programs in the second century. A standard method was to appoint two men of integrity to collect funds for the poor each Friday. They made their rounds through the market place and residences taking up gifts of money or goods for the com-

munity chest or, literally, basket. Three other men were com-
missioned to make the distribution and, when necessary, to
investigate personally the need of a family seeking charity. To
those considered to be in genuine need enough food was given
for fourteen meals, which was to last for two weeks. Special
collections might be made during the week for emergencies or
to care for a hungry traveler. Begging from house to house was
discouraged, although mendicants did make appeals to house-
wives' sympathy.[17] It was not exceptional for some beggars to
feign an illness in order to inspire pity.[18]

Jerusalem, as the center of the Jewish religion, attracted
many indigent persons and aged people, who made their final
pilgrimage in order to die in the Holy City. The religious festivals were attended by devout Jews and proselytes from far and
near who considered alms given in Jerusalem at holy times
particularly meritorious.[19] Their generosity lured both poor
and sick to the city in search of alms and even in the hope of
some miracle. Beggars concentrated at the gates and shrines
where pilgrims passed and congregated in those courts of the
temple that were not forbidden to them. Among their number
were frequently found fakes and pretenders who feigned illness
in order to receive alms. In Jesus' time Jerusalem had acquired
the reputation as a city in which many idlers lived, and a considerable portion of the proletariat derived their parasitic existence from the religious functions of the city. The Jewish historian Josephus tells how in the years prior to the destruction
of Jerusalem in A.D. 70 this rabble element roamed the streets
and terrorized the citizens. They burned the archives in order
to destroy the accounts of their debts. The revolutionary Zealots enlisted members from this lower social class, who agitated
in the civil war fought in Jerusalem prior to the fall of the city.[20]

An important group living on charity or relief was the scholars. Since Jerusalem was the center of Judaism, the most famous
rabbis gravitated there. Teachers were not paid for their instruction and so depended on the hospitality of friends or chari-

table persons. They also received assistance from the distribution of the tithes for the poor. Students contributed to their teacher's income on occasion, but they were themselves with only meager means.[21] Rabbis were forced to engage in some trade in order to provide themselves with necessities. A few acquired modest wealth, but the majority lived at best on the economic fringe or in actual deprivation. An example of the hardship that rabbis suffered is presented by R. Akiba, who had to sleep on straw in the winter. Jesus lived in this tradition of the poor teacher who "had no place to lay his head" (Matt. 8:20; Luke 9:58).[22]

The Jewish heritage provides the background against which Jesus and his followers must be understood. The historic memory of their slavery in Egypt gave the Jewish people a special concern for the poor and oppressed. This humanitarian interest gained theological support by the faith that Yahweh in his mercy had liberated them from bondage and called them to be a people for his own possession. Therefore Yahweh's merciful character should be reflected within the society. The exploitation of a brother and even a foreigner was inexcusable. In the name of Yahweh the prophets called for social justice and obedience to the covenant laws that sought to protect the weak. It is on this tradition that Jesus drew for his teachings concerning social justice. And it is the concept of the church as the true Israel and family of God that offered the first Christians a basis for their ministry to the poor.

Notes

Chapter 1

1. It will be helpful to point out for the general reader levels of historical concern that capture the attention of the New Testament scholar, although it should be recognized that these levels overlap in the actual process of research. (1) The self-understanding of Jesus is the presupposition of his message and ministry. However, earlier attempts to reconstruct the psychological development of Jesus have been abandoned because of the nature of the available sources. (2) The expression of Jesus' self-understanding in word and deed continues to be an object of historical research. (3) The context in which Jesus' ministry was performed and his interaction with his cultural surroundings in Judaism also must be investigated. (4) One must ask the question of how the first hearers and disciples understood the message and person of Jesus. (5) The meaning of these eyewitnesses was repeated to those who in turn told yet others, and forms of oral tradition developed. Not only did oral forms evolve, but the words of Jesus were kept alive by continually applying them to new situations in the church's life. The analysis of these forms and their evolution is form criticism *(Formgeschichte)*. (6) As the Christian evangelists moved from Palestine to predominantly Greek-speaking Roman provinces, the message was no longer told in Aramaic, Jesus' native tongue, but in Koine Greek, the language of the Hellenistic marketplace. (7) Some undertook to compile fragmentary accounts of Jesus' ministry prior to the writing of the Gospels of the New Testament. The discovery of traces of these earlier documents, as well as the literary relationship that exists between the Synoptics (Matthew, Mark, and Luke), falls within

the purview of literary criticism. (8) Finally, the student of the New Testament must be sensitive to the theology of the author himself: What is his historical situation, audience, purpose in writing, scheme of organization, method of redacting the sources available to him? In many respects the understanding of the author's own theological stance may prove as significant as the trustworthiness of the account that he gives.

Chapter 2

1. Compare Alfred Plummer, *The Gospel According to S. Luke*, 5th ed. (*The International Critical Commentary*, 1922), p. 6; William Manson, *The Gospel of Luke* (*Moffatt New Testament Commentary*, 1930), pp. 275–78; S. M. Gilmour, *Gospel According to St. Luke* (*The Interpreter's Bible*, 1952), 8:48.

2. Due to the doctrine of the perpetual virginity of Mary, Catholic exegetes prefer to understand ἀδελφοί as meaning "cousins" rather than "brothers," which is its primary meaning. See C. E. B. Cranfield, *The Gospel According to Saint Mark* (1959), p. 144; Ernst Lohmeyer, *Das Evangelium des Markus* (*Kritisch-exegetischer Kommentar über das Neue Testament*, 1963), pp. 8of.

3. Ezra P. Gould, *The Gospel According to St. Mark* (*The International Critical Commentary*, 1896), p. 104.

4. *Jerusalem in the Time of Jesus*, 3rd ed., trans. by F. H. and C. H. Cave (1967), p. 115.

5. See Appendix, page 90.

6. Rudolf Bultmann is correct in seeing the obvious messianic implications of riding upon an ass into Jerusalem (cf. Zech. 9:9), but he is unnecessarily skeptical in considering this account as being manifestly legendary. Bultmann, *The History of the Synoptic Tradition*, trans. by John Marsh (English, 1963), pp. 261f.; Vincent Taylor, *The Gospel According to St. Mark* (1959), pp. 451f.; Krister Stendahl, *The School of St. Matthew* (1954, 1968), p. 119.

7. Plummer, p. 215; see also W. F. Arndt, *The Gospel According to St. Luke* (*Bible Commentary*, 1956), pp. 221–24.

8. Raymond E. Brown, *The Gospel According to John* (*Anchor Bible*, 1966), 1:448.

9. Günther Bornkamm, *Jesus of Nazareth*, 3rd ed., trans. by Irene and Fraser McLuskey with J. M. Robinson (1959), p. 68.

10. Brown, 1:371; Bultmann, *Das Evangelium des Johannes* (*Kritisch-*

exegetischer Kommentar über das Neue Testament, 1964), p. 251.

11. Joachim Jeremias, *The Parables of Jesus,* 6th ed., trans. by S. H. Hooke (1963), p. 147; C. H. Dodd, *The Parables of the Kingdom,* 2nd ed. (1936), pp. 189–94; Bultmann, *Theology of the New Testament,* trans. by Kendrick Grobel (1951), 1:8.

12. Oscar Cullmann, *The State in the New Testament* (1956), pp. 20–23; and *Jesus and the Revolutionaries* (1970), pp. 47–50.

13. See the very instructive chapter, "The Rise of the Apocalyptic," in H. H. Rowley, *The Relevance of the Apocalyptic,* 3rd ed. (1962), pp. 13–53; and also chapters 10 and 11 in *The Method and Message of Jewish Apocalyptic* (1964) by D. S. Russell.

14. Bultmann, *Theology of the New Testament,* 1:11–22.

15. Gould, p. 213. Taylor does not consider Jesus' action in cleansing the temple to be revolutionary, p. 463.

16. Cranfield, "Riches and the Kingdom of God, St. Mark 10. 17–31," *Scottish Journal of Theology* 4 (September 1951): 309–13; Johannes Leipoldt, *Der soziale Gedanke in der altchristlichen Kirche* (1952), pp. 95–101.

17. For attempts to soften the hardness of this saying see Taylor, p. 431.

18. See Arnold Brooks, "Salvation and Loss in the Story of Zacchaeus," *The Expository Times* 33 (1921–22): 286–88; and Plummer, pp. 435f.

19. Appendix, p. 93; Rowley, pp. 23–27.

20. F. Godet, *The Gospel of St. Luke,* trans. by M. D. Cusin (n.d.), 2: 180.

21. Gilmour, p. 118. The Hebrew word "poor" *(anaw)* denotes primarily one who is in material need; however, *anaw* also is applied to those who acknowledge their dependency upon God, i.e., the "pious poor" (see Appendix pp. 92f.). Matthew (5:3) by adding the gloss "in spirit" suggests the latter understanding of *anaw,* while Luke's (6:20) context demonstrates that he is concerned with the economically poor in contrast to the rich. Plummer (p. 180) is correct in his judgment that in Luke: "We have no right to supply τῷ πνεύματι from Mt. It is actual poverty that is here meant. Nor is it the meaning that actual poverty makes men 'poor in spirit.' Still less does it mean that poverty is itself a blessing. There is no Ebionite doctrine here. But 'to *you,* My disciples, poverty is a blessing, because it preserves you in your dependence on God, and helps you to be truly His subjects.' " While Bornkamm (p. 76) grants that, "As Jesus uses the words, poverty and humility have their original meaning," he also seeks to explicate the

theological significance of Jesus' address to the poor. "The poor and they that mourn are those who have nothing to expect from the world, but who expect everything from God. They look towards God, and also cast themselves upon God; in their lives and in their attitude they are beggars before God." (Cf. p. 202, footnotes 21 and 23.)

22. See Bultmann, *The History of the Synoptic Tradition*, pp. 110f.; Cranfield, *The Gospel According to St. Mark*, p. 333; Lohmeyer, p. 216; F. C. Grant, *The Gospel According to St. Mark* (*The Interpreter's Bible*, 1951), 7:808.

23. Bornkamm, p. 76.

24. Joachim Jeremias, *The Eucharistic Words of Jesus*, 3rd ed., trans. by Norman Perrin (1955), p. 30.

25. Gilmour, p. 216; Plummer, p. 311.

26. H. L. Strack and Paul Billerbeck, *Das Evangelium nach Matthäus* (*Kommentar zum Neuen Testament*, 1956), 1:715; Joseph A. Fitzmyer, S.J., "The Aramaic Qorban Inscription from Jebel Hallet Et-turi and Mark 7:11/Matt. 15:15," *Journal of Biblical Literature* 78 (1959): 65.

27. Cranfield, "The Good Samaritan," *Theology Today* 11 (1954): 371f.; John Bowman, "The Parable of the Good Samaritan," *The Expository Times* 59 (1948): 153.

28. The genuineness of this pericope has been questioned often, because there are parallels to it in Jewish tradition as well as Indian and Buddhist literature. See Bultmann, *The History of the Synoptic Tradition*, p. 33; Taylor, p. 496.

29. Grant, p. 842; Bornkamm, pp. 122f.

30. Luke omits this story as contained in Mark and Matthew in favor of another similar account (Luke 7:36–50). Luke's account does not contain the statement that the poor are always with you. In John (12:1–8) the tradition has identified Judas as the one who complained about the woman's wastefulness, not because he cared for the poor, but because he stole from the money box of the twelve.

31. Dodd, *The Interpretation of the Fourth Gospel* (1960), p. 336.

Chapter 3

1. C. H. Dodd, *The Apostolic Preaching*, 2nd ed. (1944), pp. 21–23.

2. The place of origin of Luke-Acts remains uncertain but on the whole Rome appears to be the most probable location. G. H. C. Macgregor, *The Acts of the Apostles* (*The Interpreter's Bible*, 1954), 9: 22; Johannes Munck, *The Acts of the Apostles* (*The Anchor Bible*, 1967), p. lviii.

3. Tacitus *Annals* 15. 44 (Loeb); cf. Furneaux *Excursus* 2. 416–27; and Suetonius *The Lives of the Caesars, Nero* 6. 16 (Loeb).

4. I Clement 5:4–7, and Donald J. Selby, *Toward the Understanding of St. Paul* (1962), pp. 231f. See also H. D. M. Spence-Jones, *The Early Christians in Rome* (1910), pp. 7ff. and 21ff.

5. See Henry J. Cadbury, *The Making of Luke-Acts*, rev. ed. (1958), pp. 21–32.

6. Burton Scott Easton, *The Epistle of James* (*The Interpreter's Bible*, 1957), 12: 9.

7. Macgregor, p. 51; Johannes Weiss, *Earliest Christianity*, trans. by F. C. Grant (1937), 1: 56–66; Hans Lietzmann, *A History of the Church*, rev. ed., trans. by B. L. Woolf (1953), 1: 63. See also L. S. Thornton, *The Common Life in the Body of Christ*, 3rd ed. (1950), pp. 5–33.

8. Clarence T. Craig, *The First Epistle to the Corinthians* (*The Interpreter's Bible*, 1953), 10:130–35; A. J. B. Higgins, *The Lord's Supper in the New Testament* (1952), pp. 56–63; Joachim Jeremias, *The Eucharistic Words of Jesus*, 3rd ed., trans. by Norman Perrin (1966), pp. 115–22.

9. Macgregor, p. 52; Orello Cone, *Rich and Poor in the New Testament* (1902), pp. 150–58; Gerhard Uhlhorn, *Christian Charity in the Ancient Church* (1883), pp. 141–48.

10. Ernst Haenchen, *Die Apostelgeschichte* (*Kritisch-exegetischer Kommentar über das Neue Testament*, 1965), pp. 190f.; Hans Conzelmann, *Die Apostelgeschichte* (*Handbuch zum Neuen Testament*, 1963), 7: 31.

11. Haenchen, pp. 196–98.

12. Macgregor, p. 75; Haenchen, p. 188, n. 6.

13. Adolf Harnack, *The Expansion of Christianity in the First Three Centuries*, trans. by James Moffatt (1904), pp. 190ff.; W. E. Chadwick, *The Church, the State, and the Poor* (1914), pp. 15f.

14. Joachim Jeremias, *Jerusalem in the Time of Jesus*, trans. by F. H. and C. H. Cave (1969), pp. 114–19.

15. Macgregor, p. 88; Haenchen, pp. 213f.; Johannes Leipoldt, *Der soziale Gedanke in der altchristlichen Kirche* (1952), pp. 107–13.

16. These seven men are generally considered to be the first deacons. While Acts does not call them "deacons," they are said to be in charge of the "distribution," literally "service" *(diakonia)*. Their responsibility "to serve" *(diakonein)* the church demonstrates that they functioned as deacons, and Acts' use of these two cognate forms of the word "deacon" clearly suggests that this was their function.

17. Craig, pp. 84–86.

18. Fred D. Gealy, *The First and Second Epistles to Timothy* (*The Interpreter's Bible*, 1955), 11: 367–70.

19. *Ibid.*, p. 438.

20. T. G. Tucker, *Life in the Roman World of Nero and St. Paul* (1910), pp. 240–44; Tenney Frank, ed., *An Economic Survey of Ancient Rome* (1933), 1: 328–31; H. J. Haskell, *The New Deal in Old Rome* (1939), pp. 104–15; M. Rostovtzeff, *The Social and Economic History of the Roman Empire*, 2nd ed. (1957), 1: 81.

21. *The Lives of the Caesars, Nero* 6. 10; cf. *The Lives of the Caesars, Vitellius* 7. 15.

22. *Ibid.*, 6. 11.

23. *Ibid.*, 6. 12; cf. *The Lives of the Caesars, Domitian* 8. 4.

24. Suetonius *The Lives of the Caesars, The Deified Vespasian* 8. 9.

25. *Satire* 10. 78–81 (Loeb); cf. 1. 95–146. The same note is also struck by Marcus Cornelius Fronto (A.D. 100–166 [?]), statesman and tutor to Marcus Aurelius, in his *Correspondence* 17 (Loeb): "People are held fast by two things above all, the corn-dole and the shows. . . ." See also Naphtali Lewis and Meyer Reinhold, eds., *Roman Civilization* (1955), 2: 229–38.

26. Tenney Frank, *Aspects of Social Behavior in Ancient Rome*, (1932), pp. 92–117. Many descriptions given in the chapter "Rome's Experiments in Social Reform" are worthy of note in the light of more recent social trends.

27. *The Manual of Discipline* 8. 1ff., cited from Theodor H. Gaster, *The Dead Sea Scriptures*, rev. ed. (1964), p. 63; also see R. K. Harrison, "The Rites and Customs of the Qumran Sect," *The Scrolls and Christianity*, ed. Matthew Black (1969), pp. 26–36; John Allegro, *The Dead Sea Scrolls*, 2nd ed. (1963), pp. 110–33.

28. *The Manual of Discipline* 6. 1–8, Gaster, p. 57.

29. *Ibid.*, 6. 23f., Gaster, p. 60.

30. *Ibid.*, 6. 13–23, Gaster, p. 58; also see W. R. Farmer, "The Economic Basis of the Qumran Community," *Theologische Zeitschrift* (1955), Band 11, 295–308.

31. *Ibid.*, 9. 8–11, Gaster, pp. 66f.

32. Outside of Qumran, where strict communism was not practiced by the Essenes, measures were taken to provide for their own poor, especially the orphans, sick, aged, and unprotected girls. *The Zadokite Document* 14. 12–18, Gaster, p. 94; Sherman E. Johnson, "The Dead Sea Manual of Discipline and the Jerusalem Church of Acts," *Zeitschrift für die altestamentliche Wissenschaft* (1954), Band 66, 108–12; Haenchen, pp. 191f.

33. Leander Keck, "The Poor Among the Saints in Jewish Christianity," *Zeitschrift für die neutestamentliche Wissenschaft* (1966), Band 57, 77f.

34. See Matthew Black, "The Dead Sea Scrolls and Christian Origins," in *The Scrolls and Christianity*, ed. by Matthew Black (1969), pp. 97–106; A. Dupont-Sommer, *The Dead Sea Scrolls* (1956), pp. 97–100; Charles T. Fritsch, *The Qumran Community* (1956), pp. 122–25.

35. Weiss, 2: 714; Lietzmann, 1: 181.

Chapter 4

1. Ernst Haenchen, *Die Apostelgeschichte* (*Kritisch-exegetischer Kommentar über das Neue Testament*, 1965), p. 317.

2. For an exceptionally thorough discussion of the collection, see Charles H. Buck, Jr., "The Collection for the Saints," *Harvard Theological Review* 43 (January 1950): 1–29.

3. See F. C. Baur, *Paul, The Apostle of Jesus Christ*, 2nd ed., trans. by E. Zeller (1876), 1: 119–28.

4. New Testament scholars have reached no consensus in determining which visits of Paul to Jerusalem mentioned in Acts are to be equated with those visits that Paul mentioned in Galatians. The four major theories are that the visit to Jerusalem mentioned in Galatians 2 is to be identified with the visit of: (1) Acts 15; (2) Acts 11; (3) Acts 11 with Acts 15 being a doublet of the same visit; (4) Acts 15 with Acts 11 being a doublet of the same visit. See Keith F. Nickle, *The Collection* (1966), pp. 51–59.

5. There was some precedent for this collection found in the Jewish custom of sending the half-shekel temple tax annually to Jerusalem in order to support the cultic worship. Proselytes to Judaism were also expected to pay this tax. The Roman historian Tacitus complains that the "worst rascals" were converted to Judaism and immediately began to send tribute and contributions to Jerusalem (*The Histories* 5. 5). However, Paul's collection was an offering made once for the poor and not for cultic rites. See Nickle, pp. 74–99.

6. Clarence T. Craig, *The First Epistle to the Corinthians* (*The Interpreter's Bible*, 1953), 10: 256; Johannes Weiss, *Der Erste Korintherbrief* (*Kritisch-exegetischer Kommentar über das Neue Testament*, 1910), p. 381; Hans Conzelmann, *Der erste Brief an die Korinther* (*Kritisch-exegetischer Kommentar über das Neue Testament*, 1969), p. 354; C. K. Barrett, *A Commentary on the First Epistle to the Corinthians* (*Black's New Testament Commentaries*, 1968), p. 387.

7. The historical reconstruction of Paul's interaction with the Corinthian church is problematical. I have dealt with this problem in

greater detail in "Paul's Interaction with the Corinthians," *Journal of Biblical Literature* 84 (June 1965): 139–46.

8. For the possible identification of these two emissaries, see Alfred Plummer, *Second Epistle of St. Paul to the Corinthians* (*The International Critical Commentary*, 1915), pp. 247f.

9. "But beyond this, Paul understands the offering as a demonstration of a central truth: There can be no division of life into two parts, brothers in spirit but quite unrelated in such material matters as food and clothing. If Jews and Gentiles share in spiritual blessings they share as well in material blessings (Rom. 15:27)." Fred B. Craddock, "The Poverty of Christ," *Interpretation* 22 (April 1968): 170.

10. *Ibid.*, pp. 162–69.

11. Anders Nygren, *Commentary on Romans*, trans. by C. C. Rasmussen (1949), pp. 230–48; Karl Barth, *The Epistle to the Romans*, trans. by E. C. Hoskyns (1918, 1957), pp. 188–91.

12. Floyd V. Filson, *The Second Epistle to the Corinthians* (*The Interpreter's Bible*, 1953), 10: 370; Hans Lietzmann, *An die Korinther I, II* (*Handbuch zum Neuen Testament*, 1949), 9:135.

13. Plummer, p. 238.

14. Plummer, p. 363; Filson, p. 414.

15. See C. S. C. Williams, *A Commentary on the Acts of the Apostles* (*Harper's New Testament Commentaries*, 1957), p. 210.

16. Also see Richard Batey, *The Letter of Paul to the Romans* (*The Living Word Commentary*, 1969), pp. 181–83.

17. G. H. C. Macgregor, *The Acts of the Apostles* (*The Interpreter's Bible*, 1954), 9:282–84.

Chapter 5

1. The reader is referred to the significant analysis of Langdon Gilkey in *Naming the Whirlwind* (1969) in the chapter, "The Cultural Background of the Current Theological Situation."

2. Gibson Winter, "The Suburban Captivity of the Churches," *Metropolis: Values in Conflict*, ed. C. E. Elias, Jr., *et al.* (1964), pp. 79–84.

3. William Stringfellow, *My People is the Enemy* (1964), pp. 85–99.

4. Erich Fromm, *The Revolution of Hope* (1968), pp. 1–5.

5. H. H. Rowley, *The Relevance of the Apocalyptic*, 2nd ed. (1943), pp. 150–78.

6. H. Richard Niebuhr, *Christ and Culture* (1951), pp. 1–11.

7. See F. W. Dillistone, *The Structure of the Divine Society* (1951), pp. 58–69.

8. Harvey Cox, *The Feast of Fools* (1969), pp. 7–18.

Appendix

1. Von Lic. A. Kuschke, "Arm und reich im Alten Testament," *Zeits= chrift für die altestamentliche Wissenschaft* (1939), Band 57, 31– 34.

2. Roland de Vaux, *Ancient Israel, Its Life and Institutions,* tr. by John McHugh (1957, Eng. 1961), p. 68.

3. For the date of origin of the laws found in the Covenant Code, their preservation, and final redaction see Otto Eisfeldt, *The Old Testament,* 3rd ed., trans. by P. R. Ackroyd, (1964, Eng. 1965) pp. 212–19; cf. Robert H. Pfeiffer, *Introduction to the Old Testament,* 2nd ed. (1948), pp. 211–26.

4. Archaeological discoveries from Tirzah, the modern Tell el-Farah, demonstrate this social revolution. Tirzah was the first capital of the northern kingdom before Omri (c. 876–869) moved the capital to Samaria. The tenth-century dwellings are of a similar size and floor plan but the eighth-century houses show a marked contrast between the large, well-constructed homes in the rich section and the hovels of the poor crowded together in the depressed quarter. See de Vaux, pp. 72f.

5. Johannes Pedersen, *Israel, Its Life and Culture,* 1 (1926): 85–89.

6. Martin Noth. *The History of Israel,* 2nd ed., trans. by P. R. Ackroyd, (1958, Eng. 1960), pp. 269–80.

7. Eisfeldt, pp. 231–33; Walther Eichrodt, *Theology of the Old Testament,* 6th ed., trans. by J. A. Baker (1959, Eng. 1961), pp. 74–97.

8. Paul Heinish, *Theology of the Old Testament,* trans by W. G. Heidt (1955), pp. 187–90.

9. De Vaux, p. 74.

10. Ernst Bammel, πτωχός, *Theological Dictionary of the New Testament,* G. Friedrich, ed., trans. by G. W. Bromiley, (1959, Eng. 1968), 6: 893.

11. *The Manual of Discipline* 6: 13–23; 9: 8–11, in *The Scriptures of the Dead Sea Sect,* Theodor Gaster, ed. (1957), pp. 6of., 67; also see A. Dupont-Sommer, *The Essene Writings from Qumran,* 2nd ed., trans. by G. Vermes (1961, Eng. 1962), pp. 86f. and p. 94, n. 2.

12. *Jubilees* 23:18–23; *Syriac Baruch* 70:4; and Bammel, *Theological Dictionary* . . . 6: 895.

13. *Testament of Issachar* 7:5; *Testament of Joseph* 3:5; *Testament of Asher* 2:5–7; in R. H. Charles, *Apocrypha and Pseudepigrapha of the Old Testament*, 2 (1913).

14. Bammel, *Theological Dictionary* . . . 6:895.

15. *Sifrè Deuteronomy*, sections 116–18, Meir Ish Shalom, ed. (1948); also H. Strack and P. Billerbeck, *Kommentar zum Neuen Testament*, (1956), 1:346f.

16. George F. Moore, *Judaism* (1954), 2:167, n. 3.

17. See Johannes Leipoldt, *Der soziale Gedanke in der altchristlichen Kirche* (1952), pp. 62–69.

18. Moore, pp. 174–76; and Solomon Zeitlin, *The Rise and Fall of the Judean State* (1967), 2: 281–83.

19. Franz Rosenthal, "Sedaka, Charity," *Hebrew Union College Annual* 23, Pt. 1 (1950–51), pp. 411–30.

20. Josephus, *Jewish War* 2: 274–76, 425–29; 5: 442–45. (Loeb ed., 1956–57). See also Oscar Cullmann, *The State in the New Testament* (1956), pp. 8–23.

21. Joachim Jeremias, *Jerusalem in the Time of Jesus*, 3rd ed., trans. by F. H. and C. H. Cave (1962, Eng. 1969), pp. 112–19.

22. The reader who wishes to study in detail the programs of charity that developed in Egypt, Israel, Greece, and Rome should see the definitive study of Hendrik Bolkestein, *Wohltätigkeit und Armenpflege im vorchristlichen Altertum*, (1939); also see his *De Armen in de moraal, de politiek en de religie van de voor-christelijke oudheid.* (1939).

Index

Index of Biblical References

72 73 10 9 8 7 6 5 4 3 2 1

DATE DUE

NOV 12 '77			
NOV 29 '77			
DEC 13 '77			
SEP 29 '78			
NOV 28 '78			
DEC 12 '78			
F APR 19 '79			
MAY 4 '79			
8/25/81			
12/5/82			
RESERVE FALL 85			
AUG 27 '86			
F			